THE WALTER PRESCOTT WEBB MEMORIAL LECTURES: VII

ESSAYS ON
THE GILDED AGE

BY
CARTER E. BOREN
ROBERT W. AMSLER
AUDRA L. PREWITT
H. WAYNE MORGAN

Introduction by Jenkins Garrett

Edited by
Margaret Francine Morris

PUBLISHED FOR THE UNIVERSITY OF TEXAS AT ARLINGTON
BY THE UNIVERSITY OF TEXAS PRESS, AUSTIN & LONDON

Library of Congress Cataloging in Publication Data

Main entry under title:

Essays on the gilded age.

(The Walter Prescott Webb memorial lectures, no. 7)
Includes bibliographical references.
1. United States—Civilization—19th century—
Addresses, essays, lectures. I. Boren, Carter E.,
1912–   II. Series.
E169.1E785   917.3'03'5   72–8266
ISBN 0-292-72004-1

Manufactured in the United States of America
Composition and printing by The University of Texas
    Printing Division, Austin
Bound by Universal Bookbindery, Inc., San Antonio

CONTENTS

PREFACE

The seventh annual Walter Prescott Webb Memorial Lectures were held at The University of Texas at Arlington on April 13, 1972. As in preceding years, the program brought four speakers to consider various aspects of a common theme. In the vigorous years of "The Gilded Age" lie the roots of many contemporary problems. Today, as then, men try to adapt their concepts of religion and justice to a changing world; the impact of an expanding technology still confronts man and his environment.

Carter E. Boren is a theologian and philosopher. He has examined "the halcyon years" of American Protestantism in those decades at the turn of this century which concluded three hundred years of Protestant dominance. Sometimes warring sects shared an overarching aim: to "Christianize" the world. They found unity in common aims and moved vigorously to place the church in the mainstream of American society. Christian union in missionary enterprises in the west was followed by movement into the cities to meet the needs of immigrants, and urbanized society, and those displaced by industrialization in this last great surge of "Protestant America."

Robert W. Amsler, a student and disciple of Webb's, found inspiration for his essay in the "Great Frontier" hypothesis in which Webb held that the geographical frontier of the New

World had provided both an outlet and a resource for five hundred years and was an unequaled force in the shaping of the modern world. The closing of that frontier led man to seek new frontiers in science and technology. Despite many proclamations of "new frontiers" in power generation, locomotion, and communications, nowhere has there been such a universal explosion of energy since the "Great Frontier" closed. Dr. Amsler suggests that, if we use the technology of our time to seek new energy sources and to find solutions to the problems it has created, we may well discover a new concept of the nature of frontiers themselves.

Legal historian Audra L. Prewitt examines the status of the legal profession in the last decades of the nineteenth century. She finds a profession falling in public esteem and at odds with itself, as bar and bench blamed one another for the public's distrust of all lawyers and disrespect for the law itself. Radical reformers and die-hard conservatives banded together for a time in forming bar associations to police their own ranks, and more lawyers entered politics to try to bring the law and its practitioners into step with the new drummer. Her findings suggest that, as public confidence in the mechanics of justice again falls, lawyers must once more reexamine themselves and their calling.

H. Wayne Morgan, now professor of history at the University of Oklahoma, turns his attention to the late-Victorian roots of modern pollution problems. That contemporary scourge of the cities, the internal-combustion engine, was once hailed as urban man's salvation from the insanitary drudgery of removing horse manure from city streets. Industrial mechanization and cheap electricity would lift the yoke of heavy manual labor and free the common man for more intellectual pursuits. But blackened sheets on city clotheslines hinted at a problem, and pioneering legislation was aimed at cleaning skies and rivers. However, the technology of the times was not equal to the mess and, in fact, sometimes magnified it. By 1900, environmentalists recognized the problems they faced. Their failure to solve them did not come from lack of concern or imagination, but, Morgan asserts, from "the failure to question basic attitudes that promoted waste and inhibited social planning."

As president of the American Historical Association, Walter Prescott Webb spoke "history as high adventure," and addressed a wider audience than his academic colleagues. In sinewy prose, he insisted that man carries his past with him like a shadow, that he cannot intelligently consider his future without understanding his past. A man of strong convictions, he accorded to others the same intellectual freedom that he demanded for himself. In the last chapter of *The Great Frontier*, he spoke of history's field as "broad as the trail mankind has made out of the past." It is to this spirit that we dedicate this lecture series, to encourage scholars to seek out knowledge, interpret it, and present it to the widest possible audience. The Webb Lectures Committee is grateful to all those who have joined in successfully raising this memorial.

MARGARET FRANCINE MORRIS

INTRODUCTION

In this volume the very fine lectures presented at the 1972 Walter Prescott Webb Memorial Lectures are published. I commend each to you.

Recently I was asked if I thought the subject matter of the Webb Lectures in this and prior years is in keeping with what Dr. Webb would have approved in a series named in his honor. From the tone of his voice and from subsequent discussion, it was obvious that my questioner had been disturbed to find that many of the series topics were not within the literary corrals of the western movement or western history.

Even a cursory review of the content of these essays should negate any doubts that might be raised by such a question for those who identify with Dr. Webb. Professor Morgan's lecture describes the continual conflict between the Americans' desire to subdue and exploit abundant nature, their expectations of invention, progress, growth, and prosperity, and their concern for the preservation of their environment and natural resources. Professor Morgan places this conflict in a historical perspective by pointing out that such concerns were a major public question in this country as early as the turn of this century.

Professor Prewitt challenges the legal profession to undertake a reassessment of current legal concepts and relationships, and probably to do more and timely soul-searching, emphasizing the responsibility of the legal profession itself toward maintaining a judicial system responsive to the needs of the society in which they live.

Dr. Amsler discusses the new frontiers of science and technology and whether or not they will take the place of the geographical frontier, which, as Dr. Webb often pointed out, no longer exists.

Dr. Boren, after examination, concludes that the era of the predominance of Protestantism in America is at an end.

Each of these essays will be of interest to those who are curious about what happened at the turn of this century and its influence upon the species we call "man." To me, this is Webb's kind of stuff. As he wrote in an editorial which appeared in *Junior Historian*: "The function of history as I see it, is to describe and make understandable the forces which have shaped the destiny of man and brought him to the present time equipped as he now is with his ideas and institutions."

In fact, the dedication of these annual lectures to Dr. Webb lends them a limitless variety of subject matter. History, geography, science, politics, government, economics—all were among the fields Webb invaded in his compulsive drive for a more complete and satisfying understanding of man and man's bending to the influences and environment he encountered. To him, his quest was high adventure.

Dr. Webb's inaugural address as president of the American Historical Association, which he entitled "History is High Adventure," is described by his dear friend, E. C. Barksdale, as "the high water mark of Webb's shorter contributions." More than that, it represents to me a full confession and disclosure of the uninhibited scope of his quest of discovery, the cause and effect, premises and proof of his approach to history.

In my view, Webb was not a "western historian." Rather, he viewed history from the vantage point of one who, from boyhood, knew and understood how an unrelenting, arid, and treeless land did something to the man who came from the east with a determination to subdue it. Webb firmly believed the fates had been uniquely kind to him in affording him this vantage point. Birth in a particular geographical area, which Webb considered to have been so fortunate in his case, is not necessarily requisite for attaining this vantage point for observing and analyzing man and his history. Happily, the seating capacity is unrestricted. High adventure can be found there.

JENKINS GARRETT

DIVIDED PROTESTANTISM: *A Unifying Force in Nineteenth-Century American Culture*

BY CARTER E. BOREN

ONE OF THE MOST PERSISTENT CATEGORIZATIONS of American society concerns religious life and religious imperatives. Hypotheses are formulated and labeled—for example, the Puritan Ethic, or, more recently, WASP. Whether of predominantly Anglo-Saxon descent or not, the nation is certainly predominantly white and Protestant. Yet, again and again, it has been pointed out that what is distinctly American about Protestantism in America is the diversity of Protestant groups.[1] An almost enigmatic fact about our history is how American Protestantism has been able to clothe itself with any identifiable unity. Yet, a point too often missed is that, from the beginning, divided Protestantism in America has exhibited a kind of persistent unity. The diversity itself has expressed our culture as a whole.

This unity has come from a long common tradition in which Protestantism has been predominant. Near the end of the eight-

---

[1] Willard L. Sperry, *Religion in America* (Cambridge and New York: At the University Press, 1945), p. 1.

eenth century it had taken a definite form, and, for the next one
hundred and twenty-five years, America was formed in a Protestant matrix. It was the Protestant era, and, in 1950, when Arnold
J. Nash wrote the introductory chapter for a symposium, *Protestant Thought in the Twentieth Century*, he entitled it "America
at the end of the Protestant Era."[2]

After 1914, in the period of post-Protestant America, Protestantism lost its dominating influence. It had become so unified in
its divergent expressions that it sought to adjust itself to the
culture rather than to have an impact upon it.[3] A religion of
Americanism was taking the place of American religions among
Protestants.[4] The American experience did not transform either
Catholicism or Judaism is the same manner, for ties with the Old
World, racial and language barriers, and durable, definite the-
ologies impeded their complete identification with the American
cultural society.[5]

American Protestantism is so multiform that it defies treatment
as a single historical entity, and, as Willard Sperry has pointed
out, "it seems to lend itself to only a series of histories, the histories of individual denominations. In America the seamless robe
seems to have been shredded into so many rags and tatters that it
is beyond recovery,"[6] and "the religious history of the United
States is that of an ecclesiastical fecundity and fertility carried to a

[2] Arnold Samuel Nash, ed., *Protestant Thought in the Twentieth Century: Whence and Whither?* (New York: Macmillan, 1951), pp. 3–13.

[3] Ralph Henry Gabriel, *The Course of American Democratic Thought* (New York: Ronald Press, 1940), pp. 308–330.

[4] Sperry, *Religion in America*, p. 146.

[5] Winfred Ernest Garrison, *The March of Faith* (New York: Harper and Brothers, 1933), pp. 200–202.

[6] Sperry, *Religion in America*, p. 10.

point which must distress any theologically minded Malthus."[7]

Protestantism, not one but many institutions, has no single structured government or discipline, no accepted liturgy, no officially adopted creed, and no central organization.[8]

On the other hand, American Protestantism has never been as diverse as its more than 250 different religious bodies in the United States would suggest.[9] No more than 18 of more than 250 denominations can claim as many as 500,000 members; only a few of the remainder have as many as 50,000 adherents. All of the larger bodies and most of the smaller ones can be grouped together in 6 or 7 major denominational families. The larger bodies in these family groups make up over 95 percent of the Protestant church membership of the nation. As for the rest, some 200 denominations encompass only 3 percent of the nation's Protestant church membership.[10] Thus, Protestant diversity is much less complex than it appears on the surface.

We can speak of an American Protestantism, however, because Protestant churches, in spite of institutional differences, have been shaped to a common pattern, a legacy from colonial America.

Edmund Burke, in a speech on March 22, 1775, on the eve of the American Revolution, gives us the first insight into understanding American Protestantism. Said he to Parliament: "Eng-

[7] Ibid., p. 71.

[8] Winfred Ernest Garrison, *A Protestant Manifesto* (New York: Abingdon-Cokesbury, 1952), pp. 9–15.

[9] William Warren Sweet, *The American Churches: An Interpretation* (New York: Abingdon-Cokesbury, 1948), pp. 75–76.

[10] Garrison *Protestant Manifesto*, pp. 15–16; see also Sperry, *Religion in America*, pp. 75, 94, 285–287; Sweet, *American Churches*, pp. 75–96; Frank S. Mead, *Handbook of Denominations* (Nashville: Abingdon Press, 1951), pp. 185–190.

land, sir, is a nation which still I hope respects, and formerly adores, her freedom. The colonists emigrated from you when this part of your character was most predominant: and they took this bias and direction the moment they passed from your hands. They are therefore not only devoted to liberty, but to liberty according to English Ideals, and on English principles. . . . The people are protestants: and of that kind which is the most adverse to all implicit subjections of the mind and opinion. This is a persuasion not only favorable to liberty, but built upon it."[11] Burke has here used two principal words: English, and Protestant. They describe the American colonies (in spite of minor diversities of the middle group);[12] they explain the colonists' "fierce spirit of liberty,"[13] and they serve largely to explain both "the diversity and the unity of American Protestantism."[14]

The diversity was mainly a British importation. Two factors provided the unity: one, a definite Protestant tradition, Puritan Calvinistic theology, which Edmund Burke designated as the predominant "theological inheritance from abroad"; and the other, a "formative influence exerted by the American environment."[15]

True, not all of the colonists were of English descent, but most were.[16] According to Sperry, "seven out of ten of the White pop-

[11] Edmund Burke, "On Conciliation With the Colonies," in *Burke's Politics: Selected Writings and Speeches on Reform, Revolution, and War*, Ross J. S. Hoffman and Paul Levack, eds. (New York: Alfred A. Knopf, 1949), pp. 69–70.

[12] Winthrop S. Hudson, *Religion in America* (New York: Charles Scribner's Sons, 1965), pp. 5–6.

[13] Ibid., p. 6.

[14] Winthrop S. Hudson, *American Protestantism* (Chicago: University of Chicago Press, 1961), p. 3.

[15] Hudson, *Religion in America*, p. 7.

[16] Sperry, *Religion in America*, pp. 264–271.

ulation were of English blood and almost nine out of ten were British." Significant contributions were made to colonial life by non-English elements, but the prevalent pattern was acceptance of the English way of life and assimilation into the English stock.[17] Even those who were not of English descent came in time to speak of their "rights as Englishmen." Thus, the most obvious conditioning factor in American religious life was its English beginning.[18]

Not all of the colonists were Protestants. Most of them had no connection with any church. In Virginia at the beginning of the eighteenth century only one in twenty was a church member and the proportion was much smaller in the other southern colonies. William W. Sweet estimates that "one person in five at most was a church member in New England and New England was the best churched section of the colonies."[19] Of those who were connected with a church in any way, the preponderant majority were Protestant. Frank S. Mead gives the distribution of congregations as 98.4 percent Protestant, 1.4 percent Roman Catholic and .15 percent Jewish.[20]

That the American colonies were English settlements ac-

---

[17] Ibid.

[18] Hudson, *Religion in America*, pp. 5–6.

[19] William Warren Sweet, *Religion in Colonial America* (New York: Charles Scribner's Sons, 1942), p. 335.

[20] Membership statistics are not available. The relative strength is indicated by the number of congregations in each group. According to Mead, *Handbook of Denominations*, pp. 185–190, the number of congregations for 1775 were: Congregational, 668; Presbyterian, 558; Anglican, 495; Baptist, 494; Quaker, 310; German Reformed, 159; Lutheran, 150; Dutch Reformed, 120; Methodist, 65; Roman Catholic, 56; Moravian, 31; Congregational Separatist, 27; Dunker, 24; Mennonite, 16; French Reformed, 7; Sandemanian, 6; Jewish, 5; Rogerine, 3.

counts largely for the multiplicity of Protestant bodies in early America. England exported her own religious diversity, and the policy of toleration followed by the governments (both English and Dutch) with regard to new settlements accounted for the multiform nature of American Protestantism. Initial laws assuming there would be uniformity were not enforced, and, for commercial reasons, these laws were later mitigated. The exceptional attempts in New England to enforce religious uniformity failed.

All of the diversity eventually culminated in full religious liberty. By the end of the colonial period most of the churches welcomed and defended the principle of religious freedom on theological grounds. This is difficult for some people to comprehend, for it is said that one who is "willing to tolerate any religion either doubts or is indifferent to his own." Religious indifference on the part of "the unchurched liberals" greatly facilitated the achievement of religious liberty in America.[21] When Benjamin Franklin lay close to death, he responded to a question by President Ezra Stiles of Yale concerning his religious faith in this way:

You desire to know something of my Religion. It is the first time I have been questioned upon it. But I cannot take your curiosity amiss, and shall endeavor in a few words to gratify it. Here is my Creed. I believe in one God, Creator of the Universe. That he governs it by his Providence. That he ought to be worshipped. That the most acceptable Service we render to him is doing good to his other children. That the soul of Man is immortal, and will be treated with Justice in another Life respecting its Conduct in this. These I take to be the fundamental Principles of all sound Religion, and I regard them as you do in whatever Sect I meet with them. . . . As to Jesus of Nazareth . . . I think the System of Morals and Religion . . . the best the World ever

[21] Sweet, *Religion in Colonial America*, pp. 334–339.

saw or is likely to see; but I apprehend it has received various corrupting Changes, and I have . . . some doubts as to his Divinity, tho' it is a question I do not dogmatize upon, having never studied it, and think it needless to busy myself with it now, when I expect soon an Opportunity of knowing the Truth with less trouble.[22]

It is easy to see how Benjamin Franklin and all of the other church latitudinarians (deists), with their beliefs, or lack of beliefs, were willing to give the widest latitude of belief to all men.[23] The question is how others who were members of churches with specific doctrines and who were not religiously indifferent to them could also be devoted to the struggle for religious freedom.

From the very beginning, American Protestantism was characterized by a multiplicity of independent bodies, but "it was a multiplicity within an overarching unity." All these independent American Protestant churches were Christian. All of them were Protestant, heirs of that reordering of Christian traditions that took place in the sixteenth-century Reformation. Of further significance, the great majority of these churches stood within a single reformation tradition—English Puritanism—and this predominantly Calvinistic theological inheritance tended to shape the views of all the churches.[24]

A few Protestants were completely outside the Calvinist tra-

[22] Benjamin Franklin to Ezra Stiles, March 9, 1790, in *The American Enlightenment*, Adrienne Koch, ed. (New York: George Braziller, 1965), pp. 108–109.

[23] Deism did have four positive beliefs: God, Immortality, Morality, and Reason.

[24] André Siegfried, *America Comes of Age* (New York: Harcourt, Brace, 1927), pp. 33 ff.; see also James Bryce, Viscount, *The American Commonwealth*, new edition, completely revised . . . with new chapters (New York: Macmillan, 1910), I, 306.

dition, late immigrants, such as the Lutherans, Mennonites, Dunkers, and Moravians. Except for the Dutch Reformed and other minor sects, the non-English Protestants did not begin arriving until the beginning of the eighteenth century.

Anglicanism was the earliest form of American Protestantism. Dating from the settlement of Jamestown in 1607, the Church of England was almost entirely Reformed or Calvinistic in its theological outlook. The Calvinism of the *Institutes of the Christian Religion* was undoubtedly the predominant theological current. At the end of the colonial period the Reformed or Calvinist tradition as expressed in English Puritanism and the related Presbyterianism of Scotland and northern Ireland was the principal Old World religious influence. Philip Schaff, a noted church historian, endeavored to analyze this feature of American religious life shortly after his arrival from Germany in 1844. The American church, he said, "viewed as a whole owes her general characteristic features, her distinctive image, neither to the German or Continental Reformed, nor to the English Episocopal communion," but to the Puritans of New England.[25] Whatever its shape or vintage, Calvinism was the tool which shaped American Protestantism to a common pattern. Vivid similarities of practice, faith, and vision existed in the five major bodies which made up 85 percent of all the Protestant congregations at the time of the American Revolution. Whether Presbyterian, Congregational, Baptist, Episcopalian, or Quaker, all were influenced by Calvinism.

As English became the common language of all the colonists,

[25] Philip Schaff, *America: A Sketch of Its Political, Social, and Religious Character*, Perry Miller, ed. (Cambridge, Mass.: Harvard University Press, Belknap Press, 1961), pp. 54, 89, 107, 116–117.

English patterns of church life penetrated the churches of continental origin. As German and Dutch colonists joined in the American Revolution to defend their "rights as Englishmen," Presbyterian ministers were preaching in Dutch Reformed churches; Swedish Lutherans and French Reformed groups were being absorbed into the Church of England; German Lutherans were being Anglicized, Americanized, and Puritanized to varying degrees.[26] Jonathan Edwards, a Congregationalist, was elected to the presidency of Princeton University, a Presbyterian institution. Brown University, the new Baptist college, began to graduate twice as many Congregationalists as Baptists, and John Witherspoon, colonial America's foremost Presbyterian leader, could say of New Jersey at the end of the colonial period that Baptists were Presbyterians on all points save infant baptism. This Calvinist penetration caused one British visitor to say, "A thin veneer of seventeenth-century English Puritanism has been laid over the most divergent traditions."[27] The "common pattern" could hardly be cut from a thin veneer.

Forces from the Old World shaped Protestantism in the New World in a common pattern, and the American environment further unified the colonial churches. Old, established practices could not always be applied under the new conditions.[28] In the face of immediate and urgent needs, Protestant bodies were forced to improvise, adapt, and adjust. As a result, the laity

[26] Ibid. This Puritanism, or Puritan Calvinism, did not remain static in theology and is often referred to as Puritan Evangelism.

[27] The Presbyterian Westminster Confession of Faith and the Baptist Philadelphia Confession of Faith were almost identical. See Hudson, *Religion in America*, p. 44.

[28] S. E. Mead, "The American People: Their Space, Time, and Religion," *Journal of Religion* 34 (1954): 244–255.

gained a decisive voice in the direction of church matters.[29] Ministers, far removed from the ordered church life of the Old World, became dependent upon whatever support they could persuade the laity to give them in starting and maintaining churches. Among Virginia Anglican churches, control fell into the hands of lay vestries who hired the minister and determined his salary. The Congregational conception of an aristocracy of ministers having powers independent of the laity was eroded by hard-grained individualism and the severe conditions of frontier society.

All of the churches were further molded to a common pattern by the plain fact that in the new environment a new beginning had to be made; thus local church congregations were formed which tended to become independent self-governing units. They resisted later attempts to regularize them or draw them into traditional synodal, diocesan, or associational relationships.

Another influence that shaped the life of the American churches was the Great Awakening. It caught up all of the denominations. It stressed personal or conversional experience, insisting that the Christian life was not the mere observance of the outward forms of religion. Leaders of the Awakening moved from colony to colony, and George Whitefield, preaching from Georgia to New Hampshire, linked the local revivals into a single movement which affected all the churches by modifying the form of public worship, introducing a more popular type of preaching, creating new forms of architecture, and producing a new understanding of the mission of the church.

Although the revivals had their discordant notes and in some

[29] Sweet, *American Churches*, pp. 135–136.

cases did produce division, the participation of most of the churches was indispensable to the success of a revival in any community, and the net result was unity. The revivalists were aware of the potential for and danger of divisiveness, and Charles Grandison Finney, one of the greatest of the nineteenth-century revivalists, warned his aides against dwelling on sectarian distinctions and being sticklers about them.[30] On the whole, the revivals provided opportunity for Christians to work side by side and gave further impetus to cordial relations among the principal denominations.

To really understand nineteenth-century Protestant domination of American culture, one must consider still another unifying force. American Protestantism rests upon the denominational theory of the church, an American phenomenon under which "different Protestant groups claim no monopoly on the Christian word, but only a right to compete for adherents within an ecumenical Protestant community."[31] It is opposed to sectarianism,[32] for the sect thinks of itself as the only true church and claims the authority of Christ for itself alone.[33] By definition, the sect is exclusive, separate.

The word *denomination* was adopted and popularized by evangelists, in both England and America, because it implied no negative value judgment. It is a neutral, ecumenical, inclusive term. It infers that the body "denominated," or called by a specific name, is but one member of a larger group to which all de-

[30] Charles G. Finney, *Lectures on Revivals of Religion,* 2nd ed. (New York: Leavitt, Lord, 1835), p. 369.
[31] Hudson, *American Protestantism*, p. vi.
[32] Hudson, *Religion in America*, p. 81.
[33] Hudson, *American Protestantism*, p. 34.

nominations belong. Winthrop Hudson, in his *American Protes-*
tantism, is explicit: "No denomination claims to represent the
whole Church."[34]

Although used by sixteenth-century Protestant reformers and
by seventeenth-century Puritan divines, the concept of denomina-
tionalism as the opposite of sectarianism was adopted in the first
years of the evangelical revival in the eighteenth century. John
Wesley's oft-quoted words are typical: "I . . . refuse to be distinguished from other men by any but the common principles
of Christianity. . . . I renounce and detest all other marks of distinction. But from real Christians, of whatever *denomination*, I
earnestly desire not to be distinguished at all. . . . Dost thou love
and fear God? It is enough! I give thee the right hand of fellow-
ship."[35]

Gilbert Tennent, Presbyterian leader of the colonial period,
also made the same point with clarity: "All societies who profess
Christianity and retain the foundational principles thereof, not-
withstanding their different denominations and diversity of senti-
ments in smaller things, are in reality but one church of Christ,
but several branches (more or less pure in minute points) of one
visible kingdom of the Messiah."[36]

The denominational theory of the church, acknowledging the
"unity which existed within the diversity of ecclesiastical forms,"
made it possible for the diverse groups to cooperate in good con-

[34] Ibid.

[35] John Wesley, "The Character of a Methodist," in *Works, 1841*, VIII,
332–333.

[36] Leonard J. Trinterud, *The Forming of an American Tradition* (c. 1949;
rpr. Freeport, N.Y.: Books for Libraries Press, 1970), p. 132; see also Samuel
Davis, *Sermons on Important Subjects* (New York: Sexton and Miles, 1842),
I, 217–218.

science for the achievement of the great ends they had in common. It made it possible for the revivalists to respond together when it came to reaching out to the vast majority of people altogether outside the churches. The revivalist leaders went to the meetinghouses of different denominations to preach and were not unduly disturbed when their converts turned to some other denomination. This lenient attitude, although not extended to all religious persuasions, and marred by some "excesses of party zeal" and denominational rivalry, was the characteristic emphasis throughout the nineteenth century. American Protestantism was ready to conquer the forces of irreligion and to fashion a Protestant America. The problems and experiences of the post-Revolutionary era served to prove the American Protestant churches were able to do it. By the middle of the century, it was clearly demonstrated that they, to borrow the churchmen's language, could Christianize the nation, set the mores and moral patterns, and provide the foundation for commonly shared religious beliefs essential to the well-being of the Republic.

This religious experience was extended to the political realm. It was generally acknowledged that in a democracy, if laws are to be determined by a majority vote of the total citizenry for the public good, all legislative action is dependent upon individual character and personal decision. The moral order is secure and the public good advanced to the extent that a majority of the people are persuaded to adopt the wholesome laws that God has designated for the well-being of the community. Therefore, the churches, operating on the proposition that a majority of men could be persuaded to heed the public good rather than their own self-interest, put out upon a daring venture. Faced with the twin threats of "infidelity" (deism) and the barbarism of the new

1800 to 1850, and the churches were held in universal esteem. The first half of the nineteenth century witnessed some marked changes in Protestantism, in both thought and practice, but the changes did not impede the ultimate domination of American nineteenth-century culture by Protestantism. In a number of ways they helped to facilitate the Protestant role.

The Protestant coalition which had operated the complex of voluntary societies so efficiently fell apart with the collapse of the societies, beginning in the late 1830's. But the collapse was only temporary. The need for combined effort seemed less urgent, since the threat of "infidelity" was overcome, and "the problem of churching the West" was reduced to manageable proportions. A stable, churchgoing society defined in Protestant terms seemed well established, making it possible for the churches to give more of their attention to denominational concerns and denominational aggrandizement.

During the years following 1830, another far-reaching change took place. Puritan or Calvinistic evangelicalism gave way to Popular, or Arminian, evangelicalism. Now, no longer was it true, as Ralph Gabriel had once so aptly and accurately said, that "the God whom Americans worshipped was the deity to whom John Calvin prayed with such intensity of devotion and singularity of purpose."[40] For the rest of the century American Protestantism was to be defined in Methodist terms. Some church historians, and one Presbyterian church historian in particular, have called the nineteenth century "The Methodist Age in Church History."[41]

[40] Gabriel, *Course of American Democratic Thought*, p. 31.
[41] Robert Ellis Thompson, *A History of the Presbyterian Churches in the United States* (New York: Christian Literature Co., 1895), p. 34; see also

Puritan evangelicalism with its Calvinistic heritage couched in the five points of Calvinism stressed sound doctrines and a proper church order. Methodist evangelicalism stressed the conversion experience, freedom of the will, and individual morals, with hardly any doctrinal interests or implications for any proper church order. It does not refer to the Methodist per se but to a whole cluster of new ecclesiastical bodies which had defected to Methodist views and techniques: the United Brethren, the Evangelical Association, the Free-Will Baptists,[42] the Cumberland Presbyterians,[43] and the Disciples of Christ, or "Christians."[44]

Leonard W. Bacon, *A History of American Christianity* (New York: Christian Literature Co., 1897), p. 176.

[42] The best account of the origin and early history of Free-Will Baptists is found in I. D. Stewart, *History of the Free-Will Baptists, 1780–1830* (Dover, N.H., 1862), vol. I; see also *Dictionary of American Biography,* s.v. "Randall, Benjamin," by William H. Allison.

[43] John V. Stephens, *The Genesis of the Cumberland Presbyterian Church* (Cincinnati: Privately printed, 1941), pp. 103–111; Richard McNemar, *The Kentucky Revival . . . etc. Presented to the true Zion traveller . . . by Richard McNemar* (Albany: Reprinted by E. & E. Hosford, 1808), p. 27. "Minutes of the Synod of Kentucky, Oct. 15, 1802," "Minutes of the Cumberland Presbytery, Oct. 5 and 7, 1803," "Minutes of the Synod of Oct. 2, 1804," and "Minutes of the Transylvania Presbytery, Oct. 9, 1801" are in a collection of source materials in William Warren Sweet, *Religion on the American Frontier, 1783–1840* (Chicago: University of Chicago Press, 1936), II: *The Presbyterians,* 129–393; see also Robert Davidson, *History of the Presbyterian Church in the State of Kentucky* (New York: R. Carter, 1841), pp. 224 ff. See B. W. McDonald, *History of the Cumberland Presbyterian Church* (Nashville, 1888), pp. 20–25, 77–81; Samuel J. Baird, "A Collection of the Acts, Deliverances, and Testimonies of the Supreme Judicatory of the Presbyterian Church" [Philadelphia], pp. 185–186, in William Warren Sweet, *Religion in the Development of American Culture, 1765–1840* (New York: Charles Schribner's Sons, 1952), pp. 216–219.

[44] Charles Crossfield Ware, *Barton Warren Stone: Pathfinder of Christian Union* (St. Louis: Bethany Press, 1932), chap. 10; see also "Life [autobiography] of Barton W. Stone," appended in James R. Rogers, *The Cane Ridge*

Old-line churches shifted from a Puritan evangelicalism to a Popular evangelicalism, diluting their traditional Calvinism almost beyond recognition. This was especially true on the matter of "free will," where such leaders as Nathaniel W. Taylor, Lyman Beecher, Albert Barnes, and Charles G. Finney preached their way in Congregational and Presbyterian churches to a full-blown Methodism which emphasized salvation as one's own voluntary act. Complex and involved restatements of liberalized Calvinism on "free will" were made to provide for the evangelists an "effective basis for their revivalistic efforts" and shift them out of the Calvinist camp into the Methodist camp.[45]

Calvinism, with its rigid doctrine of predestination, which divided people into only two classes, the saved and the damned, had little appeal, especially to the democratic and classless society of the nineteenth-century midwestern frontier. Arminianism made all people equal in the sight of God, able to accept or reject the salvation provided for all.[46] With the democratic Jeffersonian individualism sweeping the country, Arminian evangelicalism, with its emphasis on man's participation in his own salvation, was naturally more appealing in a society where the frontiersman

---

Meeting House (Cincinnati: Standard Publishing Co., 1910), pp. 147–153, 163–170; see also Winfred Ernest Garrison and Alfred T. DeGroot, *The Disciples of Christ: A History* (St. Louis: Bethany Press, 1958), pp. 93–123.

[45] The picture of this modification of Calvinism is superbly portrayed in Sidney E. Mead, *Nathaniel William Taylor, 1786–1858* (Chicago: University of Chicago Press, 1942), chaps. 7, 8, 11, 12, and 14; see also Elwyn Allen Smith, *The Presbyterian Ministry in American Culture: A Study in Changing Concepts, 1700–1900* (Philadelphia: Westminster Press, 1962, for the Presbyterian Historical Society), pp. 220–224; and Sweet, *Religion in the Development of American Culture*, pp. 190–233.

[46] Sperry, *Religion in America*, p. 107; Sweet, *Religion in the Development of American Culture*, pp. 210–211, 225–228.

knew assuredly that his temporal salvation was in his own hands.

Some groups, such as the Consistent Calvinists or Edwardians, the Dwightians,[47] the Hopkinsonians, the Tylerites, Taylorites, Beecherites, Bushnellites, in addition to the Old Lights, the New Lights, and the New Haven (Yale), and Andover Calvinists, sought to make Calvinistic concepts more acceptable by reframing them; the result was much theological hair-splitting—elusive statements of doctrine woven of twisted chains of logic that verged on incomprehensibility. Yet, in the process, American Protestantism in the major denominations became defined almost wholly in Methodist Arminian terms for the latter half of the nineteenth century.[48]

As Calvinism was watered down, a realignment in the numerical strength enhanced the new developing unity, bringing an end to most of the surviving elements of the Puritan age. At the end of the colonial period, Congregationalists and Presbyterians had been the two largest denominations.[49] By 1850 they had been replaced by the Methodists and the Baptists. The Methodists were far out ahead with a reported membership of 1,324,200; the Baptists were second, with 815,000; the Presbyterians numbered 487,000; the Congregationalists came fourth with 197,000; the Lutherans had 163,000; the Disciples, 118,000; and the Episcopalians, 90,000.[50] The triumph of Popular evan-

---

[47] Charles E. Cunningham, *Timothy Dwight, 1752–1817* (New York: Macmillan, 1942), pp. 319, 327–328; see also Mead, *Nathaniel William Taylor.*

[48] Sweet, *American Churches*, p. 130.

[49] Charles Augustus Briggs, *American Presbyterianism: Its Origin and Early History* (New York: Scribner, 1885), p. 343.

[50] Sweet, *American Churches*, p. 42. See also C. C. Cole, *The Social Ideas of the Northern Evangelists, 1826–1860* (New York: Columbia University Press, 1954), pp. 13–14.

gelicalism, or Methodist Arminianism, provided a new bond of unity with which to face the new problems of urbanization in the latter half of the nineteenth century. Sprouting cities created a new demand for united action. The collapsed Protestant coalition was renewed with the Methodists as full partners.[51]

From the beginning of the nineteenth century, Protestantism had been the ruling "religious and cultural force" in the United States. By the middle of the nineteenth century, Protestantism indisputably dominated almost every facet of national life.[52] A Protestant America had been fashioned by the churches, and the mastery of the churches extended far outside their defined membership. For the populace at large, patterns of belief and conduct were set by the churches. While not actual members or communicants, the great majority of Americans thought of themselves as adherents of one church or another.

This Protestant dominance of the culture can be seen in many areas.[53] The American democratic faith, for instance, was set in these years on a candid, simple supernationalism based on Christian ideas as interpreted by Protestants. The middle decades of the century saw the religious press growing more rapidly than the secular press both in number of periodicals and in circulation. Even laymen read and relished the theological treatises. Revivals swept the urban centers on the eve of the Civil War, and they were approved by religious and secular observers alike with scarcely a critical voice heard anywhere. The cultural dominance of Protestantism is seen especially in the ease of transition to a

[51] Hudson, *Religion in America*, pp. 178–180.
[52] R. T. Hardy, "The Protestant Quest for a Christian America, 1829–1830," *Church History* 22 (1953): 10–12.
[53] Ibid.

public, tax-supported school system, which R. T. Hardy suggests was "palatable to Protestants because the schools were rather clearly Protestant in orientation."[54] In higher education as well, Protestants dominated. All of the American colleges, an observer in 1857 reported, with here and there an exception, were founded by religious men and turned to the interests of the churches.

This was the America the churches sought to preserve as they faced new problems after the Civil War. They succeeded well, for in spite of new, intricately complex urban problems, the halcyon years of American Protestantism lay before them. These were the decades of the turn into the twentieth century, when Protestants calmly accepted as fact the assurance that Protestantism would overcome any and all further problems. The great challenge in the first half of the nineteenth century had been to evangelize a westward-moving population. The great task in the latter decades of the century was to win and to hold the swarms of people moving to the cities.

The urban offensive initiated city mission societies, each patterned to a different urban emphasis: rescue missions, seamen's institutes, and church extension agencies. The church's urban offensive was spurred on by the Finney and Moody revivals until urban complexities made them ineffective. Businessman Dwight L. Moody forsook his commercial pursuits to systematize urban revivalism in the fashion of big business.[55] He achieved fame by exciting into action the religious forces of cities with a million or more population: Brooklyn, New York, Chicago, Boston, Philadelphia, St. Louis, San Francisco, even London and Rome. How-

[54] Ibid.
[55] Hudson, *Religion in America*, pp. 228–234.

ever, an additional and more significant instrument in the urban
offensive of the churches proved to be the Young Men's Christian
Association.[56] A British importation, it was first organized in
London in 1844; seven years later the movement had reached the
United States. Moody may have shaped and systematized urban
revivalism, but the YMCA started and promoted it.[57]

Population flowed into the cities first from the farms and
villages where the churches had most effectively shaped the life
of the total community. The move to the cities tended to relax
the emotional ties and community pressures which kept people in
the church at home. A large segment of these "backsliding"
transplanted Christians were young men in their teens. The
YMCA, like so many other agencies of Protestant action, was
designed to intercept the teen-age boy and surround him with
good influences: a room in a Christian home, prayer meetings,
Bible classes, reading rooms, employment bureaus, and lodging-
house registers.[58] The ardent members of the YMCA saw the
whole community as its mission field; not just the young men for
which the Protestant evangelical churches had initially dedicated
it. Touching many facets of urban life, the YMCA collected
funds for the destitute, provided for the sick in hotels and lodg-
ing houses, and conducted schools for poor children. As a sharp-
ened instrument of Protestant action, it engaged principally in
evangelical activity.[59] It became the arm of the church, its mem-

[56] Charles Howard Hopkins, *History of the Y.M.C.A. in North America*
(New York: Association Press, 1951).

[57] Ibid. This book depicts a phase of the movement toward unity among
Protestants. The first association was organized in London in 1844 by a group
of young salesmen. Its immediate success could be seen in the 205 local
YMCA's that had been formed by 1860.

[58] Garrison, *March of Faith*, pp. 47–48.

[59] Hopkins, *History of the Y.M.C.A.*, p. 229.

bers preaching on street corners to the unchurched of the cities, organizing Bible study groups, distributing tracts, and working in rescue missions.[60]

The YMCA mission of Protestantism, operating across denominational lines, soon became the principal medium of the churches in promoting citywide revival campaigns.[61] Moody's "businessmen's revival" of 1857–1859 grew out of noonday prayer meeting at the New York YMCA, and was picked up by other associations in other cities. The YMCA was the most immediately available interdenominational agency at the local level,[62] able to provide the necessary communitywide coordination for Moody's campaigns.[63]

The work of the churches, of rescue missions, and the YMCA reached many new urban inhabitants, but there was no systematic effort. Protestants, therefore, picked up another instrument for their offensive, an organization known as the Evangelical Alliance. The American branch was formed in 1867 to give Protestantism's unified front a program of large-scale home visitation. By 1889, as a result of the Alliance's efforts, a systematic and continuous concern for an entire community had been inaugurated in forty cities.

[60] Ibid. See also William Gerald McLoughlin, *Modern Revivalism: Charles Grandison Finney to Billy Graham* (New York: Ronald Press, 1959), pp. 200–202, 262–267; Bernard A. Weisberger, *They Gathered at the River: The Story of the Great Revivalists and Their Impact upon Religion in America* (Boston: Little, Brown, 1958).

[61] Hudson, *Religion in America*, p. 229.

[62] Ibid., pp. 229–231.

[63] Charles Alvin Brooks, *Immigration: Its Effect on America: Its Call to the Churches* (New York: Howard Benjamin, 1915), p. 8; see also H. B. Grose, *Aliens or Americans?* (New York: Young People's Missionary Movement, 1906), pp. 237, 255.

The challenge of urbanization to Protestant unified action in the nineteenth century was caused only in part by the flow of population from the farms and villages to the cities. Immigrants from abroad, a little later, presented a much more difficult problem for the churches, for they came from widely different religious traditions, bringing with them the language and cultural barriers that isolated them. Some churchmen felt that these new arrivals must be "born again of the American spirit,"[64] if the safety of the country was to be preserved. "Nothing but Christianity, as incarnated in American Protestantism," can make an immigrant a true American, Winthrop Hudson noted, in the spirit of the times.[65]

Attempts were made to solicit support for mission work among the immigrants by equating Protestantism with patriotism, yet the literature of that period manifests a truly humanitarian and religious solicitude for the poor, friendless alien. In addition to the usual welfare and relief programs, as soon as any particular national group arrived in significant numbers—Germans, Scandinavians, French Canadians, Italians, Poles, Hungarians, Czechs, Romanians, Portuguese, Russians, and others—a strenuous effort was made to provide them with a ministry in their own language. The Baptists alone provided a ministry to twenty-one different national groups in as many different languages.[66] Training institutes were organized for developing a "native ministry," and foreign-language departments were established in most theological seminaries for specific national groups. By 1900 a body

[64] Hudson, *Religion in America*, p. 245.
[65] Ibid.
[66] Aaron Ignatius Abell, *The Urban Impact on American Protestantism* (Cambridge, Mass.: Harvard University Press, 1943), pp. 182 ff.

of clergymen sufficient to the need had been trained.[67] Many of the churches became bilingual and were later assimilated within the existing denominations of American Protestantism as English-speaking churches. Many more disappeared as their memberships adjusted to American life and found places for themselves in older American religious bodies.

Protestant action developed a program of "Christian Americanization" to help the immigrant families make a successful adjustment to American life.[68] Protestant women went into the homes to teach English and to show mothers how to cook the food obtained from American stores, to help the immigrant prepare for naturalization examinations, and to give other general help.

Protestantism developed various other strategems for achieving its successful nineteenth-century dominance. One of the most creative responses to the urban challenge was the institutional church. City populations shift. Sections of a city grow old, and vacuums are left in older parts as residents and church members move to newer areas. After the Civil War, churches followed their members to the outskirts of the city, leaving the deserted areas without a ministry. Those churches that did not follow their congregations often suffered a gradual decline. By 1880 the institutional church had become the answer to the problem of ministries to the inner, older city.

An institutional church has been defined as "an organized body of Christian believers, who, finding themselves in a hard and social environment, supplement the ordinary methods of the gospel, such as preaching, prayer meetings, Sunday school, and pastoral visitation, by a system of organized kindnesses, a con-

[67] Hudson, *Religion in America*, p. 246.
[68] Ibid.

geries of institutions, which by touching people on physical, social, and intellectual sides, will conciliate them and draw them within reach of the gospel."[69]

With doors open at all hours every day, the institutional churches sought to meet the immediate needs of the depleted neighborhood. They were centers of activity, providing gymnasiums, athletic programs, evening classes, employment bureaus, public baths, medical clinics, concerts and other entertainment, day nurseries, industrial education courses, choral societies, drama and other clubs. Some of America's largest, most prominent churches became institutional and received a new lease on life. St. George's Episcopal Church in New York, for example, with only six families still in communion and ready to close its doors when it became institutional, soon numbered five thousand members. At least 173 institutional churches existed by 1900.[70] (Mark Twain described one of these churches in his "Curious Dreams and Other Sketches," 1872).

A few years later in the twentieth century, Protestant dominance of American culture declined almost as rapidly as it had risen. The social activities which were meant to serve as a way into the life of the church were so emphasized that the ideal of humanitarian service took the place of worship in the church. Many institutional churches became social agencies which other churches were called upon to support. Although these institutional churches declined in number, the humanitarian social

---

[69] Edward Judson, "The Church in its Social Aspect," *Annals of the American Academy of Political and Social Science* 30 (November, 1907): 436; see also Gaius Glenn Atkins, *Religion in Our Times* (New York: Round Table Press, 1932), pp. 69–85.

[70] Hudson, *Religion in America*, p. 301.

agencies they left behind were all part of the Protestant pattern of culture implanted upon American life.

One of the means used by Protestants to bring people into the churches and successfully place a Christian stamp on much of American culture had to be replaced in the last quarter of the nineteenth century. Revivalism, impaired by the distractions of city life, changes in intellectual climate, and a decreasing homogeneity of population was becoming steadily less effective. The Sunday schools offered the most promising alternative for recruiting church members.[71] They were plainly an interdenominational movement, designed to multiply through united effort the number of communities throughout the land where "the Christian religion reigned supreme."[72] Beginning about 1824, missionaries of the American Sunday School Union established Sunday schools for the children of the nation. After the Civil War, lay people, in a new burst of enthusiasm and eager devotion, established others. In addition to the Sunday School Union, the International Sunday School Association, a live new agency, developed and proliferated into city, county, state, and national conventions of Sunday-school workers, all espousing the cause of Protestant dominance. Various denominations were kept working harmoniously together. Efficient convention systems which became the real strength of the movement were developed. Hosts of Sunday-school workers were brought together for rallies of enlistment, training, and focal Decision Day opportunities.

The Uniform Lesson Plan was another instrument of Protes-

[71] Marianna Catherine Brown, *Sunday School Movements in America* (New York: Fleming H. Revell, 1901); Edmund Morris Ferguson, *Historic Chapter in Christian Education in America* (New York: Fleming H. Revell, 1935).

[72] Hudson, *Religion in America*, p. 234.

tant unity not less significant than the convention system. Adopted
at the National Convention of 1872, a common lesson for each
Sunday contributed to the sense of Protestant solidarity. Next
Sunday's lesson was a bond between the members of different
denominations. There was neither radio nor television, but in such
cities as New York, Chicago, Buffalo, Boston, and Cleveland as
many as eight to twelve hundred teachers would gather every
Saturday afternoon to be given preparation on the Uniform Lesson Plan for the next day.

Popularly received and supported, the Sunday school replaced
revivals as a recruiting technique for young people in their teens.
In response to the need for evangelizing and teaching adults, the
"organized class" was developed. These classes were organized
with national conventions; one of them, in 1913, was composed
of more than nine thousand classes with a membership of nearly
one million in churches of thirty-two different denominations.[73]

As the Sunday-school classes expanded into the adult field, the
International Sunday School Association instituted machinery for
promoting them, and by 1908 it was issuing certificates of recognition to as many as six thousand new classes each year, admonish-
ing them that their chief business was the winning of souls. Each
class had a slogan: Each one win one. Enthusiasm generated;
Bible-school parades became a community fixture in many places,
with the mayor and other civic leaders ensconced in the review-
ing stand. In 1910, even Congress adjourned to witness the parade of the Adult Bible Class Federation when it held its national
convention in Washington. The next year, in San Francisco, ten
thousand men, each with a Bible, marched in the parade, carrying

[73] Hudson, *American Protestantism*, p. 121.

banners and singing hymns and official delegation songs. The entire public procession was graced by a platoon of mounted police riding at its head. All the various specifically urban agencies were reporting evidences of real strength, and, at the end of the century, the YMCA was still counting its converts by the thousands each year.[74]

The Sunday school placed principal reliance on its Decision Days for adolescents, organized classes for young adults, and Bible classes for adults. As the churches looked to the future, the Sunday schools gave them what seemed to be real grounds for optimism. They enjoyed popular support; they enlisted the ablest leadership of the community; they were vigorous and strong.[75]

These decades at the turn of the century have been called "the halcyon years of American Protestantism," and also "the great age of the American pulpit." Protestants, confident and assured, shared the general cultural conviction of the time that they were living in the best of all possible worlds. They took pride and satisfaction in achievements which they could back up with evidence. New and costly church edifices were being built. Churches were crowded; programs were multiplying; and a wide spectrum of humanitarian concerns elicited a broad range of interest and generous support. Never before had the members of the churches manifested so contagious an enthusiasm. Never before had they been so busy. It was a period of crusades which channeled the abundance of zeal and moral idealism generated by the church into good causes. The preachers were again re-

[74] For a more cautious interpretation of the effectiveness of the YMCA, see Hopkins, *History of the Y.M.C.A.*

[75] *The Sunday School: The Lyman Beecher Lectures on Preaching in Yale University* (New Haven: Yale University Press, 1888), p. 142.

garded as "first citizens" and often wielded an influence "more powerful than that of the Layman."[76] There was a whole galaxy of stars of national and international reputation whose sermons were front-page news in the daily press. Many had their entire sermons regularly syndicated throughout the nation.[77]

Perhaps it should not be surprising that this Protestant confidence and enthusiasm did not limit itself to the United States, but spilled out into the world as America became world-conscious in the later decades of the nineteenth century. Not only America but the whole world was to be Christianized. For three decades after 1886 the Student Volunteer Movement enlisted the ablest men and women on the nation's campuses to go to the far corners of the earth. The laymen's missionary movement, of a little later origin, challenged laymen to match the devotion of youth with a dedication of American Protestant dollars.[78] The emissaries of American Protestantism went to distant regions of the globe, establishing churches, building hospitals, founding schools and colleges, and transmitting the culture and institutions of the West. Thus, the Protestant resurgence in America in the nineteenth century was part of a larger movement. Its accomplishments caused Kenneth Scott Latourette to designate the nineteenth century "The Great Century" in his seven-volume history of Christianity. Only by a repetitive refrain of superlatives in the

[76] James Bryce, "A Classic Study of American Society," in the author's private library.

[77] Ibid.

[78] By 1900, although immigration had set up large communities of Roman Catholics in the cities, it was still believed these would in some way be assimilated into Protestantism; but, in fact, the flood tide of immigration during the last two decades of the nineteenth century and the first fifteen years of the twentieth century meant the end of the era of Protestant dominance.

various volumes could he describe what had taken place in the nineteenth century. "Never before in a period of equal length had Christianity or any other religion penetrated for the first time as large an area as it had in the nineteenth century,"[79] he said, and "never before had any religion been planted over so large a portion of the earth's surface."[80] "Never before had Christianity, or any other religion been introduced among so many different peoples and cultures."[81] "Never before had so many hundreds of thousands contributed voluntarily of their means to assist the spread of Christianity or any other religion."[82] "Never before . . . had Christians come so near the goal of reaching all men with their message."[83] "Never had it exerted so wide an influence upon the human race."[84] "Measured by geographic extent and the effect upon mankind as a whole, the nineteenth century was the greatest thus far in the history of Christianity."[85]

The turn-of-the-century era witnessed many new and disturbing problems. Popular skepticism caused by new scientific theories found a stalking image in Robert G. Ingersoll, but Protestants kept faith that the specter would go away.[86] A broadening tide of immigration had built up large communities of Roman Catholics in the cities, and annexations of territory had incorporated others, but it was confidently believed that "all minority groups

[79] Kenneth Scott Latourette, *A History of the Expansion of Christianity*, 7 vols. (New York: Harper & Bros., 1937–1945), V, 4–69.

[80] Ibid., IV, 1.

[81] Ibid., p. 4.

[82] Ibid., VI, 443.

[83] Ibid., VII, 450.

[84] Ibid., VI, 442.

[85] Ibid., V, 4–69.

[86] Bryce, "A Classic Study of American Society."

could be assimilated or Americanized."[87] The whole mood and spirit of the country was Protestant. It was Protestant America. These outward indications were deceptive. The so-called halcyon years of Protestantism of the two decades bridging the turn from the nineteenth into the twentieth century actually marked the end of an era. The accumulated momentum from the past was largely spent.

[87] Hudson, *American Protestantism*, p. 126.

SCIENCE AND TECHNOLOGY:

New Frontiers in the Late Nineteenth Century

BY ROBERT W. AMSLER

IN PURSUING THE STUDY OF HISTORY, I enrolled in Dr. Walter Prescott Webb's course, "Frontiers and Democracy," in which we investigated Frederick Jackson Turner's thesis that, about 1890, the frontier in the United States had disappeared. Webb extended this thesis, pointing out that the geographical frontier had ceased to exist not just in America, but everywhere, and that any new frontier would have to be nongeographical in nature. New discoveries and developments in science had been occurring with increasing frequency during the 1800's and had been put to work by technologists to better man's condition. With the disappearance of the geographical frontier, where but in the area of science and technology could one look for a new one?

The nineteenth century saw the beginnings of a number of developments. The possibilities and potentials of electricity and petroleum began to be realized; new discoveries led to inexpensive steel production. Profound changes took place in transportation and communication, and great progress was made in preventive and remedial medicine. Increased life expectancy and better health during this extended span were among the dividends paid by the application of new scientific discoveries to medical practice.

These generalizations touch a few of the new potentialities opened to Americans during the 1800's. Measuring their impact on society is more than difficult—it is impossible. I am reminded of a printed sign above the battery commander's desk in a unit with which I served during World War II: "The difficult we do immediately; the impossible takes a little longer." This impossibility takes more time and space than I have at my disposal. We may, however, pay some attention to a few of the developments that affected American society and brought about so many changes in so many lives.

Although the emphasis in this short treatment will be confined to the latter part of the nineteenth century, it must be remembered that there were some remarkable developments which occurred earlier in the 1800's. A few of these should be given some attention before the more intensive examination is begun.

One fact may be pointed out at this time: certain basic work, such as producing improved maps and instruments, had to precede the actual explorations and discoveries in the opening of the geographical frontier. This is equally true in the case of the frontiers of science. The electromagnet, for example, was employed in any number of inventions—inventions which could never have been completed without it. The first crude electromagnet had been devised by William Sturgeon of England. Joseph Henry took the idea and principle and conducted countless experiments until he had established the basic formulae for electromagnetism and was able to construct magnets of varying size and force.[1] Using one of these in a demonstration, he constructed a telegraph some five years before Samuel Morse completed his instrument.[2] Electric motors, generators, and transformers all have as their heart and soul the electromagnet or some application of it. Joseph Henry, certainly, was a pioneer who helped open a new area for technologists and inventors.

Patented in the 1830,[3] the electromagnetic telegraph enabled communication for the first time in the history of mankind to exceed the speed of transportation. The network of wire over which the telegraphic messages clicked their way began to reach almost every settlement and community.

The development of the railroad paralleled that of the telegraph. Beginning about 1830, steam railroading expanded much faster than steamboating, inaugurated some twenty-five years earlier. Steam railroading revolutionized land transportation. The work of Robert Stevens, Moncure Robinson, Horatio Allen, Matthias Baldwin, and many other pioneers speeded the development of an industry which helped meet and to an extent solve some of the problems presented by the geographical frontier. These two major breakthroughs, the railroad and the telegraph, using inorganic power, shrank both distance and time for expanding America.

Some forty years later, another development in communications was to occur, one which would more directly affect a vast number of people. The telegraph could be handled only by a trained and practiced operator; the average individual could not

[1] Roger Burlingame, *Scientists behind the Inventors* (New York: Hearst Corp., Avon Books, 1960), pp. 47–50.

[2] Ibid., p. 51.

[3] Melvin Kranzberg and Carroll W. Pursell, Jr., eds., *Technology in Western Civilization*, 2 vols. (New York: Oxford University Press, 1967), I, 454.

himself use it. Would it be possible ever to *talk* to a person some distance away—to have a two-way person-to-person conversation? Several inventors and technologists were working on the idea, including Alexander Graham Bell, Elisha Gray, and Thomas Edison. The first to achieve success was Bell, who presented himself, his plans, and a working model of the telephone to the U. S. Patent Office, and started the application for his patent on its way. This patent, granted in 1876, has been described as the most valuable single patent ever issued. It was the beginning of a new age in electrical communications technology.[4]

There is a rather interesting note to this story in that on the same day that Bell entered his patent application, February 14, 1876, and only a few hours later (two hours to be exact), Elisha Gray came to the patent office with his plans, to enter his application.[5] The machine he would enter was almost identical to that of Bell and in fact was slightly better in performance. Although he and Bell had the same ideas and had produced essentially the same machine, neither knew anything of the work of the other. For Gray the expression "an hour late and a dollar short" would have to be rephrased "a few hours late and several million dollars short." Bell's patent was completely cleared only after extended and bitter litigation.[6] The significance of the telephone is beyond estimation. The number of instruments and the miles of wire, cable, and microwave relays employed in telephonic communication truly stagger the imagination.

[4] John W. Oliver, *History of American Technology* (New York: Ronald Press, 1956), p. 437.
[5] Richard Shelton Kirby, Stanley Worthington, Arthur B. Darling, and Frederick Gridley Kilgour, *Engineering in History* (New York: McGraw-Hill, 1956), p. 344.
[6] Ibid.

At about the same time that Alexander Graham Bell was completing the invention of the telephone, other inventors were beginning to work on additional application of electricity for man's benefit. In 1878 Charles Brush had already produced and begun to market a generator and the electric arc light, a source of brilliant illumination.[7] The arc light, a little too complicated, expensive, and dangerous to use to light a home, was being used to light public and commercial areas, and for other purposes. Thomas Alva Edison, among others, felt that a practical way to light the home by means of electricity could be found, and his effort to perfect an incandescent lamp eventually paid off. The idea was not original with him—many others had worked on it without success.

Contrary to popular belief, Edison was not a scientist in the strict sense of the word. Roger Burlingame says: "Thomas Edison thought of himself as an inventor, not a scientist. He had no real scientific education of the sort which made Joseph Henry and Willard Gibbs into great men of science. His talent was ingenuity; his success came from the infinite patience that is needed for repeated trial and error with solid materials. He was little concerned with the laws of physics."[8]

Edison's patent on the incandescent lamp in 1882 was only a part of his program for home lighting. He built an improved dynamo, plus a parallel—and later a three-wire—wiring system. He sold the homeowner a package containing dynamo, wiring, and bulbs to light his house. Thus the era of electric lighting was under way. But one more major contribution came through Edison's efforts: the central power station, generating electric

[7] Kranzberg and Pursell, *Technology*, I, 565.

[8] Burlingame, *Scientists*, p. 10.

current which was available wherever wires could be attached to the transmission lines through a meter. According to John W. Oliver, "The opening of the Pearl Street Central Station in 1882 in New York City marked the beginning of the electrical age."[9]

Although the electric light was the first and for some time the most dramatic use to which enormous amounts of electricity were applied, the development of the electric motor, and the uses to which it would be put, must be given some attention. The amount of electricity used for power far exceeds that used for lighting, even in the home, if it is equipped with air conditioning, refrigerator, washing machine, and central air heating.

Initially, before George Westinghouse started (and finally won) the battle of the currents, all motors were direct-current drive and would not operate on alternating current. Westinghouse employed Nikola Tesla, a brilliant Croatian scientist who had immigrated to America, to design a motor for alternating current. Tesla and several other scientists developed AC motors of amazing versatility, and the rest of the history of electrification is a well-known story.[10]

Although the use of electric light and power caused something of a revolution in the home, in the factory, and in transportation, its effective use in the field of medicine is almost as startling. The uses for electricity in medical practice seem limitless. Professor Oliver sums it up briefly as follows: "The incandescent lamp made it possible to explore the interior parts of the human body. The electrolytic needle was being used before 1900 to eradicate birthmarks, remove surplus hair, and to decompose malignant tumors. Electromagnets were used to extract small pieces of metal

[9] Oliver, *History of American Technology*, p. 351.
[10] Ibid., pp. 354–355.

from the eye. High voltage currents were used to anaesthetize any portion of the body to lessen pain and to excite paralyzed muscles. The electric motor was being used by dentists to operate their drills, and Roentgen's X-ray was hailed as one of the greatest contributions in all medical history.[11]

The physician is indebted to a European for the discovery and development of the X-ray. In 1895 Wilhelm Konrad Roentgen, using a Crookes tube, discovered the properties of the mysterious rays that it produced, and called them X-rays, because they were unknown.[12] The miracle of X-rays enables the diagnostician to work more wonders and arrive at his conclusion far faster than ever before.

The discoveries which made radio and television possible were made before the turn of the century. Had Thomas Edison been a true scientist, the field of electronics might have been opened much earlier. Some of his first light bulbs became discolored at their base by a bombardment of escaping electrons. Although he noted this, he did not investigate it. It remained for a number of notable scientists to make successive contributions to the exciting new phenomenon. The frontier of electronics was opened, however, and the pathfinders and explorers and trailblazers in this new area made life far more interesting than it had been in the past.

Certainly Americans cannot claim preeminence in the field of electronic development during the early period. Heinrich Hertz, who announced that he could produce and detect electromagnetic waves, was German.[13] There were many explorers and pioneers,

[11] Ibid., p. 359.
[12] Mitchell Wilson, *American Science and Invention* (New York: Bonanza Books, 1954), p. 331.
[13] Kirby et al., *Engineering*, p. 334.

just as there had been in the opening of the Great Frontier, or New World. Joseph John Thomson, who discovered the electron, was an Englishman; so, four hundred years earlier, was John Cabot. Guglielmo Marconi, the developer of the first wireless telegraph, was an Italian; so was Christopher Columbus. There would be Americans in the picture, to be sure, but they would appear somewhat later. Just for example, however, one could mention such names as Lee de Forest, R. A. Fessenden, and E. H. Armstrong, whose contributions brought into being practical radio and, later, television.

At the time that electricity was beginning to flex its mighty muscles, bringing light and power to America, developments in another field were helping build the country. Two men, an ocean apart, came up with the same principle, which would make possible the manufacture of machines and structures that before this time could be achieved only in dreams. In 1847 William Kelly, experimenting in his iron foundry in Kentucky, blasted air through the molten iron in his furnace. The air oxidized or burned most of the carbon in the iron, thus turning the brittle iron into steel.[14] By careful timing of the "blow" the carbon content could be determined and the quality of the steel controlled. Later systems provided for the introduction of such elements as chrome, vanadium, and nickel, among others.

Less than ten years later, Sir Henry Bessemer in England did exactly the same thing. Why, one may ask, is the process called the Bessemer process, when Bessemer's demonstration was years later than Kelly's? The answer to this is that Bessemer created the machinery for effective production—his converter was de-

14 Ibid., p. 294 .

signed for easy use in blast steel manufacture, and all steel produced in such converters is called Bessemer steel. Kelly had patented the process, and Bessemer had patented the converter; an
agreement was necessary and was achieved to permit both to share
royalties paid by the steel foundries being built. The more efficient and flexible open-hearth system of steel production made
its appearance in the 1880's, and steel, unlimited, was on its way.
Historians consider the rapid rise of the steel industry one of
the most important aspects of the Industrial Revolution in the
nineteenth century.[15]

Obviously, many scientists and technologists, as well as a few
entrepreneurs, made valuable contributions to the growth of the
steel industry. Time simply does not permit their inclusion,
though they richly deserve recognition. The mighty Carnegie
combine and the even more colossal empire of United States Steel
give some indication of the magnitude and importance of steel
production.

Just as the wheels of industry's machinery were ready to start
turning as never before, and just as the supply of whale oil
seemed to be diminishing, thus dimming the lamps in America,
a new material, petroleum, was introduced to grease the wheels,
oil and power the machinery, and light the lamps of the country.
Petroleum, of course, was not really new. It had been known
since antiquity, and there were a few areas in America where it
had seeped to the surface of springs and streams, even collecting
in small puddles. The Indian had been curious about it and had
tried it out in various ways. He found that it was not edible, that
it smelled bad when he smeared it on himself, and that it made

15 Ibid., p. 298.

too much smoke when it burned. Although he used it occasionally in flares when it was convenient, he largely ignored it.

The shortage and the increasing price of whale oil as an illuminant was causing many of those connected with the business to wonder about the possibility of another source of oil. The extraction of an illuminant from coal had been improved to the point of being practicable, and the cost of distillation and refining was being lowered. Benjamin Silliman, Sr., as early as 1833, had demonstrated the feasibility of similarly treating the "rock oil" recovered from springs and seeps,[16] and A. C. Ferris was producing illuminating oil commercially, though on a small scale, in the late 1850's,[17] but, quite obviously, petroleum could never make any significant contribution to the total supply of illuminants as long as no greater supply existed than the amount available from surface seeps.

Benjamin Silliman, Jr., was hired to run an analysis and make a report on petroleum usage, the report going to a partnership initiated by George H. Bissell. Bissell had become interested in the oil skimmed from a creek near Titusville, Pennsylvania. The report was quite optimistic, and a company was formed to explore the possibility of securing and refining crude oil.[18]

The new company, with headquarters in New Haven, Connecticut, hired E. L. Drake to go to Syracuse, New York, to familiarize himself with salt-well boring, and then to go to Titusville and perfect title to the desired property. Drake had no technical experience, having been in turn a clerk, an express

[16] Harold F. Williamson and Arnold R. Daum, *The American Petroleum Industry, 1859–1899* (Evanston: Northwestern University Press, 1959), p. 68.
[17] Ibid., pp. 59–60.
[18] Ibid., pp. 65–72.

agent, and more recently a railroad conductor.[19] He had only two visible qualifications for the task: he was immediately available, and his expenses would be minimal since he could get a railroad pass.[20] In Titusville he acquired the title and "commission" he would carry for the rest of his life. Unless one lived in Kentucky, it was not easy to become a colonel, but Drake, through no effort of his own, gained that distinction. James M. Townsend, president of the company, had mailed some legal papers to Drake at Titusville, to be held until his arrival. Realizing that a little showmanship could help impress the local people, Townsend addressed the papers to *Colonel* E. L. Drake. The townfolk were suitably impressed, and Drake liked and kept the title.[21]

It is not certain who originated the idea of drilling a well. George H. Bissell claims the distinction, but it could have been Townsend (otherwise why the instruction to Drake to familiarize himself with the procedures for salt-well boring?), or it could have been Drake's idea. In any event, Drake was no expert driller; it took him almost two years to go down 69½ feet, the depth of his Titusville well. But, to quote from Williamson and Daum, "whatever Drake's shortcomings as a driller, businessman, or entrepreneur, he was the first to demonstrate that petroleum could be drilled for and obtained in substantial quantities. By this demonstration he removed the major barrier to the rise of a new industry."[22]

Drake had encountered many difficulties, among them a reluctance on the part of the company to send enough money for the

[19] Paul H. Giddens, *The Birth of the Oil Industry* (New York: Macmillan, 1938), pp. 48–49.
[20] Williamson and Daum, *American Petroleum Industry*, p. 75.
[21] Giddens, *Birth of the Oil Industry*, p. 49.
[22] Williamson and Daum, *American Petroleum Industry*, pp. 76–80.

equipment and to pay the wages of the small crew of men doing the work. In fact, the company decided that the whole project should be abandoned, and, in August, 1859, sent Drake a final remittance with which to pay off all obligations, instructing him to end operations. Had there been faster postal service, the birth of the oil industry would not have occurred in 1859, but the orders to close down did not arrive until after the first oil boom in history was under way. On Sunday, August 28, 1859, the driller, "Uncle Billy Smith, looking into the top of the drilling casing, saw some sort of fluid had risen to within a few feet of the top of the pipe. Improvising a ladle, he scooped some out. This was it—OIL!"[23] The days of skimming and scraping oil seeps were ended.

Drake's success started a veritable rush of drillers to the Titusville area. Some used the most simple methods of exploration; others, highly sophisticated techniques. Although at the time the search was for a source for illuminating oil, subsequent developments would make all of the derivatives important. Internal-combustion engine fuels, many grades of lubricants, and the residue, either paraffin or asphalt, are now regarded as essential. Without them, much of man's world would shudder to a grinding halt. Drillers were soon busy in many parts of the world.

Three of the products we have examined (steel, electricity, and oil) were combined in a late-nineteenth-century development, the automobile. The steam-powered horseless carriage had been tried, but with little success. With steel for a boiler shell and kerosene or gasoline as a fuel, a lighter and more practical steam car was possible; in addition, a gasoline-consuming internal-

23 Ibid., p. 81.

combustion engine could now be made and used to power a vehicle. George Selden held the patent for such a machine, but Ransom Olds, Elwood Haynes, and the Duryea brothers all built automobiles before 1900, with Vinton, Packard, and the incomparable Henry Ford entering the field shortly after the turn of the century. "America on wheels"—a delightful idea—was possible only because of steel for construction, electricity for ignition, and gasoline for fuel to make the wheels roll.

Man's life has been improved and enriched through developments in the generation and utilization of electricity, the processing of steel, and the search for and use of petroleum. His burdens have been somewhat eased, his productivity expanded, and his increased leisure time has been made more enjoyable. Opportunities for more progress in these and additional areas unquestionably existed at the end of the nineteenth century. If the geographical frontier represented merely opportunity for expansion, then science would seem to have provided a new frontier.

An examination of our nicely developed thesis discloses several flaws, however, and some cold hard facts emphasize them. The opening of the Great Frontier or New World gave to existing western civilization a tremendous *new* supply of land, with all of its resources practically intact. It added to the known supply of nature's gifts to mankind. There were now new and fertile fields to till, new forests to cut and use, and new supplies of ore to mine. There were new plants and new animals. All of these elements were suddenly added to what already existed. Columbus and his immediate followers were responsible for this immense bounty. Since his time, up to and including the present, explorers have been probing, mapping, and charting, until practically every square foot of the surface of this planet is known. Where man can live and prosper, he is doing so. We must reiterate what has already been said: the geographical frontier is gone.

Can it be said with validity that the scientific and technological developments completed by the end of the nineteenth century really opened a new frontier? Did they present civilization with a tremendous addition to the known resources of the earth? Did the scientists and technologists give any new area—any new land to grow more crops, any new ore fields, or any new forests? Was there suddenly new room for man to increase his population and continue to feed, clothe, and house it adequately? The improvements in communication and transportation, new uses for and increased generation of electricity, knowledge of the extraction, refining, and usage of petroleum, developments of processes for cheap production of steel—did these really present the benefits that are given by a geographical frontier? To answer these questions properly, we must look at what we have already examined, but from a different point of view.

It becomes increasingly evident that the scientific frontier, or the frontier which might be opened by science and technology, has definite limitations. Except in a narrow sense, it cannot present mankind with any more usable land. It *can*, through proper use of fertilizer and irrigation, make a given area of land produce two or even three times what it formerly grew, and it can continue to do this; so the production from this land can be greatly enhanced, thus amounting to an increase in land supply. Knowledge of synthetic fertilizers and proper irrigation systems was developed before the twentieth century began, and has increased steadily since that time.

The generation of electricity involves an external power supply, and with the exception of the hydroelectric dynamos, this means a consumption of fuel. Steam turbines usually and diesel engines occasionally drive generators to create the easily transported and extensively used form of power and energy. The turbines or engines use coal, fuel oil, or natural gas to fire their boilers or push their pistons. In short, energy is most frequently produced by the destruction of fossil fuels; these fuels are not unlimited in quantity. Each weight of coal, volume of gas, or liquid measure of petroleum, once used, is gone. Since these were geologic ages in preparation, mankind does not have time to wait around for their renewal. There is an end to these resources, and new discoveries of proven reserves do not alter that fact.

Steel production involves processes which require tremendous heat, which is obtained by burning fossil fuel under blast, or by the continuous electric arc, formed by massive charges of electricity. Here, again, prodigious amounts of energy are expended to maintain steel production at its necessary level. As for the raw material going into steel production, the situation is not too critical, as scrap is used in steel in an ever-increasing ratio which can, if necessary, be stepped up.

In the third area examined, however, the new-frontier picture begins to fall apart. It is true that new methods of oil extraction and refining opened vast reservoirs of fuel to heat, generate power, light lamps, and provide lubrication for turning axles and wheels. And this was in addition to that already available, true, but, unlike many elements of the geographical frontier found in the New World, it was not renewable, but fixed. The amount available is what was there to begin with, less what has been used. What science and technology did here was to provide a faster way of getting this fuel out of storage and into use. Science did not open a new frontier but simply made available another treasure of the Great Frontier.

It is in the general field of the production of energy that the frontiers of science fail to materialize, or have failed to, almost to the present time. By the end of the nineteenth century scientists and technologists had really devised systems of depleting, rather than of adding to, the energy-producing resources of the planet earth. Further, they were beginning to pollute the atmosphere and water in the process.

To solve the problem of future energy production we need, first, a list of the sources of energy presently known, specifying which will eventually disappear and which are constant, or self-renewable. The source most extensively used at the present can be classified as fossil fuel: oil, coal, and natural gas. This source, as has been noted, is exhaustible and, for practical purposes, irreplaceable. Moreover, at the present, there is greater demand and depletion than in any other peacetime period. Presently the oil pumping allowable in Texas is at 100 percent; a power shortage is feared, and all available fuel will be needed.

A source which is very nearly constant is tidal power. A few sites are known where the tides are high and the land forms permit damming bays or inlets to install hydroelectric generation. The Bay of Fundy in Canada is an excellent example of such a site. Solar radiation is also a tremendous energy source; but the varying availability, the lack of storage facilities, and the difficulty of producing effective collecting machinery have precluded any great use of it. Wind energy has long been used, turning windmills for some few purposes, such as water pumping and grain grinding, but it is too unreliable for consistent and industrial use. There is a very considerable potential in the power of the wind, but, as in the case of solar energy, storage facilities are lacking. Geothermal energy is available in only a few locations, and cannot be counted as a major contributor to the total field.[24]

There are two remaining major sources of energy, each deserving a somewhat more extensive treatment than the preceding. One of these is water power, presently used, but certainly not to its full potential. It is estimated that only about 5 percent of the total potential of water power in the world is developed; in North America some 19 percent is being put to use.[25] On this continent, then, some five times as much hydroelectric power as is now generated could be produced. The first practical large hydroelectric turbine generators were installed at Niagara Falls by George Westinghouse in 1895.[26] The extensive use of power from these generators proved the importance of such an operation, and further installations were encouraged. Water power is constant, and it is not upon its use exhausted or diminished in quantity. When the fossil fuels become scarcer and much more expensive, the expansion of hydroelectric generation will almost certainly occur. The work of Westinghouse and his colleagues may be said to have added something to the total.

The greatest hope for the future is nuclear energy. Admittedly, it was not developed in the nineteenth century, but again, the groundwork was there. The discovery of the electron had opened a whole new field for investigation. This is stated very plainly in the book, *Engineering in History:* "[Joseph John] Thomson's

[24] Kranzberg and Pursell, *Technology*, II, 275.
[25] Ibid., pp. 284–285.
[26] Kirby et al., *Engineering*, p. 364.

discovery of the electron was the first physical evidence that such particles exist in nature, and together with the discovery by Antoine Henri Becquerel (1852–1908) of radioactivity in the previous year, 1896, forms the starting point for the remarkable development during the twentieth century of the science of atomic physics."[27]

It may well be argued that nuclear reactors require the use of raw material—uranium. While this is true, science has developed also the breeder-reactor, which, while producing energy, generates plutonium, which is itself fissionable and thus available for further reaction. Additional experiments have been and will be continued; in the opinion of many experts, the atom will, in the not too distant future, be the leading energy source in most of the world.[28]

Scientists may have come up with the answer to the problems of energy production—production without depleting the resources of the earth. If so, they have eliminated part of the need for a new frontier, or, to put it another way, they may have presented a part of a new frontier. The belief in this is perhaps best stated in the words of the publisher and editor of *Scientific American*, Gerard Piel, who writes: "The sources of energy open to nuclear physics—the oceans and the crust of the continents—are essentially infinite. The supply of materials, through the permutations and combinations of organic chemistry, may now be sought in the perpetually renewable resource of the soil."[29]

[27] Ibid., p. 335.

[28] Kranzberg and Pursell, *Technology*, II, 275. See also Albert Q. Maisel, "The Big Push to Atomic Breeder Reactors," *Reader's Digest* (April, 1972), pp. 164–168.

[29] Gerard Piel, *Science in the Cause of Man* (New York: Random House, Vintage Books, 1964), p. 150.

Dr. Louis Rayburn, professor of physics at The University of Texas at Arlington, informed me that at a conference recently at Oak Ridge a number of physicists were optimistic about the development of thermonuclear energy, using deuterium as a primary element. Since deuterium is present in and can be separated from sea water, there is an almost infinite supply of raw material available.[30]

Walter P. Webb was right, of course. The Great Frontier is gone. It is gone, and one must agree that there is no similar new frontier. The title of this essay is something of a misnomer in that respect. However, a compromise may be reached which should satisfy even Dr. Vannevar Bush, director of the (United States) Office of Scientific Research and Development. As Webb points out, Bush's book, *Science: The Endless Frontier*, comes close to promising the world a new frontier.[31] Let us say that what science offers represents a new concept of a frontier, or a new type of frontier, one which can offer much of what the geographical Great Frontier had to offer. If this can be accepted, then it may be said that the encouraging of the study of science and technology may well be the major hope for the future of all mankind.

[30] Louis A. Rayburn, personal interview, April 10, 1972.
[31] Walter P. Webb, *The Great Frontier* (Boston: Houghton Mifflin, 1952), p. 289.

BAR VS. BENCH: *New Fears*
in an Old Relationship

BY AUDRA L. PREWITT

DATE: 1831

SPEAKER: Alexis de Tocqueville, a French visitor to the U. S.,
          author of *Democracy in America*

"If I were asked where I place the American Aristocracy, I
should reply without hesitation that it is not composed of the rich,
who are united together by no common tie, but that it occupies the
judicial bench and the bar."[1]

DATE: 1870

SPEAKER: A lawyer

OCCASION: A private meeting to organize the New York City
          Bar Association

"We are here simply concerned with ourselves, and not with
the judiciary. . . . This bar has been reduced to a mere collection

---

[1] Alexis ne Tocqueville, *Democracy in America*, 2 vols. (New York: Schoc-
ken Books, 1961), I, 328.

of individuals without class or rank—a dull, dreary level of enforced equality."[2]

Forty years had witnessed drastic changes in the position of the
legal community.

Drastic as they were, even greater changes were in store. The
following three decades saw increasing abuse heaped upon the
profession that had contributed twelve presidents of the United
States, nine vice-presidents, twenty-four secretaries of state,
twenty-five secretaries of the treasury, nineteen secretaries of war,
and sixteen secretaries of the navy. In the post–Civil War decade,
lawyers were almost entirely excluded from some state legislatures. They were ridiculed in the newspapers and even barred
from joining a labor union.

The declining status of lawyers was concurrent with profound
change in the social structure of the nation as, in the last quarter
of the century, urban populations grew much faster than rural,
and political power shifted from the farm to the city. The period
saw a decline in the importance of the independent small businessman, the growth of giant monopolies, the control of political
power by bosses and professional politicians, the development of
farm and labor organizations, and the emergence of a full-scale
reform movement. An increase in the number of newspapers
and a new aggressive journalism meant more complete coverage
of this fragmented society.

Institutions which had evolved in an agrarian society were unable to perform adequately their functions in the new society.
Never had United States citizens held their government in such

[2] Henry Nicoll, "Lawyers in Council—Bar of the City of New York," 1
Albany L.J. 220 (1870).

low esteem. They were unable to comprehend that the old agrarian structure could not accommodate the impossible demands heaped upon it. The resultant problems were often explained in the time-honored method as "unique failures in leadership."[3]

Certainly the lawyers would have to answer. Lawyers in the legislature had made the laws; lawyers defended clients against law made by lawyers; lawyers on the bench administered the law made by lawyers in the legislature. The *New York Graphic* suggested ridding politics of all lawyers, then there would be none "to hocus-pocus and bedevil the law which they were paid to interpret."[4] A legal journal commented that there was no subject of newspaper comment that received "more editorial attention and less editorial justice than the legal profession."[5]

Criticism of lawyers was not new in American history. The very nature of their profession places them on the firing line. They must defend unpopular as well as popular causes, and popular opinion often tars lawyer and client alike with the same brush. But the degree and extent of criticism were new.

The legal profession had long claimed credit for the success of American government. It had pointed with pride to the number of lawyers in the constitutional convention, to the number of lawyers that had held the highest offices in the land, to the influence of lawyers in state legislatures and on the local level. It had taken credit for the past success of the structure of government; now it was receiving much of the blame for the inadequacies. As the extent of popular distrust became obvious through news-

[3] Robert M. Wiebe, *The Search for Order, 1877–1920* (New York: Hill and Wang, 1967), pp. 5–6.

[4] Quoted by A. B. McEachin, "Lawyers in Politics," Alabama State Bar Association, *Proceedings of the 12th Annual Meeting* (1890), p. 53.

[5] "The Newspapers and the Legal Profession," 9 *Albany L.J.* 81 (1874).

paper attacks and the exclusion of lawyers from the political arena, the legal community became defensive.

The *Albany Law Journal* in 1872 defined the first law of life as self-preservation, noting that the few bar associations in existence had been formed for "protection and self-preservation."[6] Later, in an 1876 discussion of "Current Topics," it called for lawyers to unite and protect their interests.[7]

The professionalization of the bar had begun. The New York Bar Association of 1870 was but the first. The American Bar Association was formed in 1878, and by 1900 there were nearly 300 bar associations in existence.[8] Codes of ethics were written, degree plans for law schools were revised, and attempts were made to regulate the type of men admitted to the bar. All of these changes seemed to be based on the premise that the discredit of the legal profession was the fault of the profession. This charge was stated bluntly by a commencement speaker at the Law School of the University of Maryland in 1874: "I speak plainly—not because so to speak is virtuous or seems to be, but because your profession is growing in discredit, and I fear deservedly, and because its regeneration must come from within and not from without."[9]

All of the proposed reforms were needed, but a segment of the bar did not accept the charge that the legal profession had itself to blame for its troubles. Speaking at a dinner in New York in 1874, David Dudley Field, one of the most famous lawyers

---

[6] "Professional Organization," 6 *Albany L.J.* 233 (1872).

[7] "Current Topics," 13 *Albany L.J.* 423 (1876).

[8] American Bar Association, *Report of the 23d Annual Meeting of the American Bar Association* (1900), pp. 644–665.

[9] S. Teakle Wallis, "Address Delivered before the Law School of the University of Maryland," 2 *Am. L. Rec.* 659 (1874).

of that day, noted that all history would bear witness that the law and the lawyers were inseparable, and the power of one rose and fell with the other.[10] If so, then the writer in the *Albany Law Journal* was correct in saying: "Much of the decadence of the legal profession . . . is really due to the defects in the law itself. So long as the people feel that a system is radically defective . . . that system must continue to decline."[11] A president of the Illinois Bar Association phrased it differently: "It is the concurrent testimony of all history that no country has ever maintained itself long in healthy prosperity when the people felt they were not safe under the law."[12]

In the new wave of introspection, the duty of the lawyer seemed now twofold: improve the quality of lawyers and improve the law. Closer examination of the latter showed that most dissatisfaction lay not with the law but with the uncertainties and delays in the law. The answer was clear: improve the administration of the law. What caused delay and uncertainty in the administration of law? An answer was readily apparent: the failure of the courts. The courts were the instrument through which law was applied, therefore, the courts were not adequately performing their tasks.

This explanation was accepted by many, and nearly every bar association set up a Permanent Committee on Delays and Uncertainties in the Law. More and more articles appeared in the legal periodicals decrying the inefficiency of the courts. Discussing the 1883 riots in Cincinnati, one writer presented a flat indict-

[10] David D. Field, "The Law and the Legal Profession," 10 *Albany L.J.* 322 (1874).

[11] "Scientific Basis of Law," 7 *Albany L.J.* 323 (1873).

[12] B. S. Edwards, "Annual Address of the President," Illinois State Bar Association, *Proceedings of the 9th Annual Meeting* (1886), p. 35.

ment: "Out of 71 prosecutions for murder and manslaughter in the courts of Hamilton County during two years ending June 30, 1883, four resulted in acquittal, two in quashed indictments, six in imprisonment, and 59 were still pending. Of such a paralysis of justice, the logical result is anarchy. No wonder that a desperate populace trampled under foot the laws that had no longer any claims on their respect."[13]

David Dudley Field was more eloquent in his accusation: "We are boastful people. We make no end of saying what great things we have done, and are doing, and yet behind these brilliant shows there stands a spectre of halting justice, such as to be seen in no part of Christendom. So far as I am aware, there is no country calling itself civilized, where it takes so long to punish a criminal, and so many years to get a final decision between man and man. Truly may we say that justice passed through the land on leaden sandals."[14]

But even as lawyers turned to the courts, a question of definition arose. Was the problem only technical? Were the courts as an institution failing to meet the demands of a changed society? If so, the institution had to be made more efficient. Perhaps more speed was the solution. The remedies were then obvious: more courts, more judges, better techniques, and fewer technicalities. Seymour Thompson, editor of the *American Law Review*, suggested less worry about process: "Popular opinion, as echoed by the press, is filled with the gross misconception that it is the right of accused persons to be tried with technical precision and formality. It is the right of an accused person to be acquitted if he is

[13] "Criminal Justice in Cincinnati," 18 *Am. L. Rev.* 675 (1884).
[14] Quoted by E. Callahan, "Annual Address of the President," Illinois State Bar Association, *Proceedings of the 13th Annual Meeting* (1890), p. 45.

innocent, and convicted if he is guilty. Beyond this, all rights which relate to modes of procedures are not his right, but the rights of society."[15]

Although few lawyers would deny that the court structure needed improvement, a concern about the judiciary was also apparent. Under "Current Topics" the *Albany Law Journal* had voiced the problem in 1870: "It is a matter of history that so long as the courts of a country maintain their integrity and independence, the rights of the people are safe but when judges become political partisans of the dominant power . . . anarchy is imminent and popular rights in peril."[16]

A judge more fully stated the relationship: "Law, with us, is an abstraction. It is personified in the courts; but its success depends upon the moral conviction of the people. When confidence in the courts is gone, respect for the law itself will speedily disappear and society will become the prey of fraud, violence and crime. In this country the power of the judiciary rests upon the faith of the people in its integrity and intelligence. Take away this faith, and the moral influence of the courts is gone and the popular respect for law impaired."[17]

A commencement speaker at the University of Michigan Law School stressed the same theme: "The reputation and influence of the bar suffer in many places through lack of public confidence in the courts."[18]

[15] Seymour D. Thompson, "More Justice and Less Technicality," 23 *Am. L. Rev.* 55 (1889).

[16] "Current Topics," 1 *Albany L.J.* 197 (1870).

[17] "Newspaper Contempt of Court," 6 *Albany L.J.* 354 (1872), quoting the opinion of C. J. Lawrence in *People vs. Wilson and Shuman*.

[18] C. A. Kent, "Commencement Address before the Law School of the University of Michigan," 7 *Albany L.J.* 217 (1872).

There could be little doubt that such fears had merit. From all over the country came accounts of intimidation and political control of the judiciary and of many questionable, if not dishonest, actions by judges. As many lawyers accepted the fact that the judiciary had, in many areas, declined in quality, they turned to debating the WHY.

These lawyers agreed that the cause was to be found in the vast changes in society. For many members of the legal community the fault was in the influence that the masses now held, the result of popular election of judges. Such lawyers feared "the passions, the prejudices, the hasty impulses of the people." The growing success of such reform movements as the Grange or Farmers' Alliances in electing their "approved" slates of judges confirmed their fears.

For others, the villain was a type of legislator who catered to the new class of wealthy industrialists. Edward Rand, speaking before a New Hampshire Bar Association in 1884, presented some impressive statistics: "There are 76 senators, and a recent census of them shows that not less than 20 are millionaires while enough more are the representatives of millionaire corporations . . . to bring up the number who may be properly styled millionaire senators to full half the whole number."[19] If this situation existed in the most august body in the country, what must have been the make-up of state legislatures?

As for the power of the press and the sensationalists of the new yellow journalism—would not the constant criticism of the bench by the press intimidate judges, cause young lawyers to

[19] Edward Rand, "Address before the Grafton and Coos Counties Bar Association," Grafton and Coos Counties Bar Association [New Hampshire], *Proceedings of the 2d Annual Meeting* (1884), p. 71.

avoid the bench and respected judges to resign due to constant harassment? Then there was always the original problem. If the quality of the bar was low, how could one expect quality on the bench?

Once the cause was determined, the cure was evident. If popular election was at fault, then appoint. If appointment was at fault, then elect. If the unlicensed opinions of the press were the cause, then restrict the press. To improve the quality of the bench, improve the quality of the bar.

The defects of these cures were obvious. Judges could be influenced whether selected by appointment or by election. Freedom of the press was guaranteed by the constitution and any attempt to restrict the press could cause more problems than it would solve. As for improving the quality of judges by improving the quality of lawyers, it was at best a gamble. Lawyers or judges are only human, with weaknesses and prejudices always present.

The legal community agreed that there was no perfect solution, no way to guarantee an honest judge or to protect judges from influence or political intimidation. Most lawyers chose the solution or combination of solutions that seemed the lesser evil: appointment, election, long terms, short terms, higher salaries, better qualifications. But while the merits of each solution were being debated by lawyers in bar association meetings and in print, one segment of the legal community considered an entirely different approach. For these lawyers, the amount of power held by the judiciary was appalling. The power of judicial review was an accepted part of judicial power. But what of judicial discretion, for example, in the writ of habeas corpus, the power to punish for contempt or libel, or the power of the injunction? Technical processes, too, gave the court immense power: con-

tinuances, qualification of jurors, time of trial, admission or re-
jection of evidence, granting or refusing new trials—all matters
within the discretion of the court. If a judge so desired, he could
delay justice indefinitely. In many states the judge had the power
to disbar a lawyer.

An anonymous writer in the *New Jersey Law Journal* of 1880
commented that the late nineteenth century would "be remembered as the age of judicial government," charging that in no
other nation or age had the courts exercised such power over
public affairs.[20] Another member of the legal community warned
that a "blind reverence for the bench is dangerous and degrad-
ing—one of the most serviceable aids to tyranny."[21]

Almost every topic of concern in legal reform found the fears
present. Newspapers, in their criticism of judges, found that
some lawyers welcomed "the glaring light of criticism as protection against tyrannical and corrupt judges." Proponents of a plan
to codify the law with uniform rules, regulations, and statutes
could depend on support from those who thought such a plan an
excellent way to limit judicial interpretation and power. Attempts
to reform or abolish the jury process were blocked by lawyers who
saw the jury as a "bulwark against the tyranny of the judges."
Striking labor unions found lawyers arguing against the use of
the injunction, charging that the injunction was an extension of
the judicial power. Farmers had unexpected allies in lawyers who
tried to stop judges from aiding failing railroads, protesting that
court direction of economic concerns was an arbitrary use of
illegal power.

[20] A.Q.K. [pseud.], "The Power of the Judge in Politics," 3 *N.J.L.J.* 39
(1880). Also quoted in 14 *Western Jurist* 207 (1880).
[21] "Submission to Law," 12 *Albany L.J.* 84 (1875).

These court powers had long existed. History was replete with instances of poor judges. The growing distrust of judicial power and judges emanated from changes in society. Concentrated wealth and popular reform movements now had more influence in politics and in the selection of judges than the lawyer had. At the same time, the growth of bar associations and the increased number of newspapers and legal periodicals meant increased communication and knowledge of the actions of judges on every level. Unable to trust judges, unable to protect and guarantee judicial honesty and independence, many lawyers seemed forced into an attack on the powers of the judiciary. But even as the legal community questioned, proposed, and argued local or state problems and sought solutions for the question of courts and judges, the late 1880's witnessed a shift of emphasis.

As local and state complaints concerning inequalities and injustices made their way to the national level, the bar was compelled to focus attention on the federal judiciary. The same problems existed at all levels. If lawyers distrusted the emotions and judgment of farmers on the state level, what could be their reaction to the third-party Populist movement of 1892 on the national level? If a portion of the legal community distrusted concentrated wealth, what difference the level—whether state or national?

By the end of the 1880's the combination of militant laborers and agrarian crusaders posed a counterthreat to the consolidation of capital. The Democratic and Republican parties seemed unable to envisage or unwilling to acknowledge the problems of the day, but, as the conflict between reformers and capitalists showed up on court dockets, the federal judiciary was forced to act.

The judiciary made its position crystal clear as decision after decision supported the rights of property owners. Circuit courts took control of bankrupt railroads with subsequent favoritism for the directors or owners. They refused to allow rival railroads to decrease rates in competition, and they used the injunction weapon against labor.

As reaction against the federal courts grew, within the legal profession and within society, the bar attempted to find the villain and a solution. As before, many lawyers saw the main concern as growing distrust of the courts. These lawyers agreed that judges had assumed too much power; the judiciary was not only interpreting laws, it was setting limitations on the power of the legislatures to enact laws. As early as 1889, John S. Frink told New Hampshire's Grafton and Coos Counties Bar Association that: "The power of the judiciary is almost unlimited. It invades both the other departments of government, as well as holds individual rights in the 'hollow of its hand.' "[22]

Cures ranging from impeachment of the Supreme Court justices to popular election of the federal judiciary were proposed, but few lawyers supported weakening the federal judicial power. Although dissatisfaction with the decisions of the judiciary was apparent, other factors had to be considered.[23] For most lawyers the first consideration was the independence of the federal judiciary. Many lawyers disapproved of the court decisions but feared the consequences of disrupting the "third and equal branch of government" concept. Furthermore, the extreme

[22] Hon. John S. Frink, "Address," Grafton and Coos Counties Bar Association [New Hampshire], *Proceedings of the 7th Annual Meeting* (1889), p. 541.

[23] For a good discussion of this aspect, see Arnold Paul, *Conservative Crisis and the Rule of Law* (Ithaca, N.Y.: Cornell University Press, for the American Historical Association, 1960).

conservatism of the federal judiciary seemed to be balanced by the excesses of the reformers and radicals. Most lawyers seemed to feel that a choice had to be made between the two extremes.

As a depression of 1893 deepened in 1894–95, the two extremes became more evident. While farmers, laborers, and the unemployed reacted in strikes and marches, the Supreme Court ruled against the Sherman Antitrust Act as applied to manufacturers, but sanctioned its use and the injunction against labor organizations, and ruled against a graduated income tax. Certainly the anti-court provisions contained in the Democratic platform of 1896 would have considerable influence on fears within the legal community. Probably the major part of the legal community aligned itself with the courts, either because of philosophical agreement, or as the lesser of two evils because it feared the consequences of social unrest from below. But a small, vocal group took a different path. These lawyers wished to correct the inequities within the structure. Although some were sincerely concerned over the injustices in society, most of their subsequent legal agitation was based on self-interest—the old fear that gross public dissatisfaction with the courts could result in disrespect for the law, violence, the ultimate destruction of the courts, and a corresponding diminution of the legal profession. In 1889, Walter B. Hill told the American Bar Association: "In the storm and stress of pending social agitations, the American people will have need to appeal to the sentiment of 'reverence for law.' Woe unto us, if disaffected agitators can retort with truth, 'Your law is not worthy of reverence.' "24

---

24 Walter B. Hill, "The Federal Judicial System," American Bar Association, *Proceedings of the 12th Annual Meeting* (1889), p. 301; other examples of this fear may be found in the following: "One Law for the Rich and Another for

The reformist lawyers did not agree on social philosophy, but they did agree that the courts were assuming too much power,[25] and that changes, good or bad, in philosophy and governmental activity should be decided by the legislatures. One spoke for many when he wrote: ". . . the safe and permanent road toward reform is that of impressing upon our people a far stronger sense than they have of the great range of possible harm and evil our system leaves open, *and must leave open* [author's italics] to the legislatures, and of the clear limits of judicial power. . . . Under no system can the power of the courts go far to save a people from ruin; our chief protection lies elsewhere."[26]

In a similar vein, Stephen Allen, in his presidential address to the Bar Association of Kansas, said, "Let the People again take to themselves the full and absolute sovereignty which is their right and the Federal Courts will cease to be looked upon with eyes of jealousy as a thing foreign and unsuited to a republic."[27]

The legal reformers realized that the courts could not be forced to change position without endangering the structure of society, and their purpose was to save that structure. Alleging acts of both

---

the Poor," 2 *Case & Com.* 40 (1895); William Aubrey, "Mob Law," Texas Bar Association, *Proceedings of the 16th Annual Meeting* (1897), pp. 126–148; "Respect for the Law," 32 *Am. L. Rev.* 109 (1898); "Lynching: How Far the Courts Are Responsible for Its Prevalence," 33 *Am. L. Rev.* 596–598 (1899).

[25] John McClure, "Our English-Bred Judges," Arkansas Bar Association, *Proceedings of the 7th Annual Meeting* (1888), pp. 14–34; Seymour D. Thompson, Alabama Bar Association, *Proceedings of the 13th Annual Meeting* (1890), pp. 88–125; "Notes," 29 *Am. L. Rev.* 427 (1895); T. W. Brown, "Due Process of Law," 32 *Am. L. Rev.* 1–30 (1898).

[26] James B. Thayer, "The Origin and Scope of the American Doctrine of Constitutional Law," 7 *Har. L. Rev.* 156 (1893).

[27] Stephen Allen, "The Federal Judiciary," President's Address, Bar Association of Kansas, *Proceedings of the 15th Annual Meeting* (1899), p. 66.

commission and omission, they placed responsibility for the problems at the door of the legal profession. It seemed incumbent, then, upon the lawyer to reexamine the purpose of his profession and the relationship between law and justice, between legality and morality, and to take the lead in readjusting political control and the execution of the law in order to correct the social problems that rendered the judiciary vulnerable. Thus, Franklin A. Wilson addressed the Maine State Bar Association: "There is no doubt that every citizen owes a duty to the public; the character and degree of duty is not the same at all. It is commensurate with opportunity and circumstances. We are lawyers; we assume we know the law, and we owe it to ourselves and to our profession to throw our influence in the direction of making good laws, and aiding in their execution. If bad laws have crept into our body of laws, repeal them; if good, execute them."[28]

Much of the blame for the extreme division within society was placed on the cooperation between lawyers and property owners. It was charged that wealth had debauched the profession, that its members accepted fees to watch out for the interests of wealth before legislative bodies, and that "a calling generally condemned when termed lobbying became respectable when called 'watching a client's interests.' "[29] Seymour Thompson con-

[28] Franklin A. Wilson, "Annual Address of the President," Maine State Bar Association, *Proceedings of the 3d Annual Meeting* (1895), p. 30. See also George H. Smith, "Of the Certainty of the Law and the Uncertainty of Judicial Decisions," 23 *Am. L. Rev.* 699–718 (1889); James C. Carter, "The Ideal and the Actual in the Law," American Bar Association, *Proceedings of the 13th Annual Meeting* (1890), pp. 217, 245; William B. Hornblower, in Georgia Bar Association, *Proceedings of the 12th Annual Meeting* (1895), p. 72; Herbert Knox Smith, "The Failures of Municipal Government," 5 *Yale L. J.* 26–29 (1895).

[29] Thomas H. Franklin, "Judicial Centralization," Texas Bar Association, *Proceedings of the 12th Annual Meeting* (1895), pp. 59–60.

demned the Senate as little "better than a collection of lawyers and agents for corporations."[30]

Lawyers urged their legal brethren to regain a position of leadership in politics and work for "good" laws, laws that accepted "the conditions of this generation" and not those of "generations dead and buried centuries ago."[31] Seymour Thompson warned that a continued disregard for the people could bring about the destruction of the structure.[32] In March of 1894, *The Bar*, a legal periodical representing the West Virginia bar, asked, "What are we here for but to go into politics?" and announced that when every lawyer in the state had read its publication "there will be a new power in politics, in legislation, in every public movement, because the profession will then be able to move together against evil and in favor of every reform demanded by the times."[33]

John W. Akin perhaps best presented the fears and desires of these legal reformers in his presidential address before the Georgia Bar Association in 1898 when he said:

Our danger lies not in criticism of the courts. Unfounded criticism reacts upon itself. To silently endure evils, to utter no protest against illegal power, to lift no voice of warning against approaching danger, is neither wise nor patriotic. Anarchy and blood will not come from timely notes of alarm against usurping encroachments of either the executive, the legislative or the judicial departments of government. What is most to be feared, because most dangerous, is that this repub-

[30] Seymour D. Thompson, "Address before the Bar Association of Kansas," quoted, 29 *Am. L. Rev.* 760 (1895).

[31] J. J. Willett, "The Case Lawyer," Alabama Bar Association, *Proceedings of the 16th Annual Meeting* (1895), p. 63.

[32] Seymour D. Thompson, "Government by Lawyers," Texas Bar Association, *Proceedings of the 15th Annual Session* (1896), pp. 64–85.

[33] "Will It Go into Politics?" 1 *The Bar* 31 (1894).

lic will quietly submit to powers assumed against the spirit of our Constitution and the genius of our government. Repression is the mother of revolution. Let all the people in all the States be aroused in time to peacefully, *and by the forms of law,* prevent and overthrow despotism, in whatever form and by whatever name, before it becomes so strong that only revolution can end it. The enemies of liberty, the real anarchists, the real criminals, are those rich and powerful, who by obtaining from the courts more than justice for themselves, and giving through the courts less than justice to others, make these courts the object first of popular suspicion, then of popular condemnation, and finally, of popular wrath.[34]

The inflation of 1897 and the economic activity and new imperialism generated by the Spanish-American War of 1898 helped ease the social tensions. The United States entered the twentieth century in a relatively peaceful mood. But the lesson had been learned; the fears could not be forgotten. The legal community of the late nineteenth century must be credited with a reassessment of legal concepts and relationships, and with laying the foundation for an organization that is vital in present-day society. The lawyers would again become a major force in politics. The legal reformers would be in the forefront of the progressive reform movement of the first years of the twentieth century.

Many of their concerns are with us today: law and order and respect for law. Once again popular sentiment seems to doubt that justice will come from the courts. Perhaps it is time for the profession to examine again its concept of law, the relationship between its institutions and popular sentiment, and the responsibility of the legal community.

[34] John W. Akin, "Aggressions of the Federal Courts," President's Annual Address, Georgia Bar Association, *Proceedings of the 15th Annual Meeting* (1898), p. 85.

AMERICA'S FIRST ENVIRONMENTAL
CHALLENGE, 1865–1920

BY H. WAYNE MORGAN

THE EFFORT TO CONSERVE America's natural resources was a major public concern at the turn of this century. Reactions to new problems in man's relation to the total environment were less obvious but equally significant. The problems of pollution, waste, and the efficient use of resources were new to industrial America but were widely discussed. Concern for the environment rose from a larger desire to regulate economic expansion and to comprehend technological change. Environmental problems were usually perceived as side effects of industrialism.

Efforts to deal with these new problems encountered deeply held beliefs about the national purpose and about the individual's relation to society. Americans accepted the idea of man's perfectibility and assumed that rational analysis, combined with science, would solve any problems arising from material development. The populace believed firmly that an ever-expanding economy was vital to the accommodation of individual talent. Americans assumed that their country was unique and could control industrialism, just as it was apparently solving other problems which had long baffled the Old World. Alexis de Tocqueville and other foreign commentators had long since noted that Americans also equated novelty with improvement, the new with the good, and change with progress.

These ideas implied that men should do all things which were technically possible, lest the momentum of progress falter. Americans believed in a beneficent future. "In America, the future is not an indefinite apprehension," one analyst noted, "it is an ardent expectation: a promise not only of ample prosperity, but of a fuller, more interesting, more satisfying life."[1] Americans were concerned not merely to make money, but to lessen labor, and to expand the range of material and intellectual choice for the individual. This attitude was the basis of consumerism. And the late nineteenth century seemed to be the first generation in man's history when most people could reasonably expect to become affluent in a burgeoning industrial order.

A tradition of weak government also hampered any systematic approach to complex environmental problems. Conflicting legal jurisdictions combined with the country's size to thwart scientific regulation of resource use. And the great majority of Americans, who did not face these new problems personally, hesitated to enlarge government power.

Changes in the environment were most obvious in the process of urbanization. The influx of population into well-established cities, such as New York, or into new cities, such as Chicago and Denver, created sudden demands on the environment. With few guiding precedents, the people who managed cities relied

[1] Hamilton Wright Mabie, *American Ideals, Character and Life* (New York: Macmillan, 1913), pp. 307–308.

on technology and experimentation. The supply of water was perhaps every city's most pressing problem. Urban governments quickly learned how to treat, store, and deliver huge quantities of pure water.[2] Public-health officers warred relentlessly against bacterial pollution, but their aim was safe drinking water. They did not conceive of any shortage that improved technology such as dams, conduits, and treatment plants could not correct. And, except for a few scientists, planners did not understand the hazards of altering ecological balances while damming rivers.

In due course, a body of experience and statistics arose, trained experts emerged from the new universities, and states and municipalities established research bureaus to study water problems. Some of these men warned against pollution's effects on recreation, esthetics, and health.[3]

Industry was the greatest water polluter, pouring wastes into recently pristine rivers and lakes. Most critical experts shrewdly attacked pollution as a form of financial cost. They tried to formulate means of turning waste materials into salable goods, and emphasized long-term savings to business in preventing pollu-

[2] Samuel W. Abbott, "Public Hygiene in the United States," in Nathaniel Southgate Shaler, ed., *The United States of America*, 3 vols. (New York: Appleton, 1894), III, 1226–1248, is a good contemporary summary. Nelson Manfred Blake, *Water for the Cities* (Syracuse: Syracuse University Press, 1956), focuses on the problem in the early nineteenth century.

[3] Paul Hansen, "The Control of Stream Pollution," *American City* 10 (January, 1914): 65–69; F. H. Newell, "Pollution of the Potomac River," *National Geographic* 8 (December, 1897): 346–351; George E. Waring, Jr., *Modern Methods of Sewage Disposal* (New York: Van Nostrand, 1896), pp. 41 ff. Two technical handbooks show the early technology available for water treatment: William Mayo Venable, *Methods and Devices for Bacterial Treatment of Sewage* (New York: John Wiley and Sons, 1908); and George W. Rafter, *Sewage Disposal in the United States* (New York: Van Nostrand, 1894).

tion.[4] State and local regulatory agencies, such as the model pioneer body in Massachusetts, combined the carrot and the stick, requiring prevention controls while doing research on the uses of effluents.[5]

In general, the treatment of industrial pollutants was minimal, though some areas of special concentration, like the Atlantic Coast and the Great Lakes, boasted many research facilities and regulatory agencies. And some pollution seemed inevitable. Water was the natural and cheapest solvent for most industrial wastes, and the nation's huge river system seemed able to carry them safely to a still larger ocean. Other forms of pollution were accidental. Water flowing through mine shafts fouled rivers with oils and minerals. Tons of allegedly soluble mercury entered Alaskan rivers as part of the gold-extraction processes used during the great strikes of the 1890's.

Of the ancient elements, air was second to water in public concern, and not only in the expanding industrial cities. Agricultural investment increased dramatically near urban areas, especially in dairy, poultry, and truck farming. As such industries as rock-crushing, cementmaking, and smelting invaded the countryside, farmers complained of the effects of chemicals on crops and animals. Arsenic and other poisons passed from smokestacks to

---

[4] "Waste Water from Factories," *Engineering Magazine* 18 (March, 1900): 915–916.

[5] "The Pollution of Streams by Manufactories," *Engineering Magazine* 22 (February, 1902): 774–775; Peter Austin, "The Utilization of Waste," *Forum* 32 (September, 1901): 74–84; "How Waste Is Turned into Money," *Scientific American* 95 (October 6, 1906): 245–246; John S. Billings, "American Inventions and Discoveries in Medicine, Surgery and Practical Sanitation," Smithsonian Institution, *Annual Report, 1892* (Washington: Government Printing Office, 1893), p. 619.

growing crops or stored feed, sometimes with disastrous results to livestock.[6]

Unlike the man in the street, experts understood that this air pollution was an international concern.[7] They studied foreign regulations and appealed to foreign precedents to prove that regulation of air pollution was both possible and feasible. Other experts analyzed the effects of smoke and airborne acids on daily living.[8] Militant crusaders graphically described the actions of air pollution: "The evil effects to town air on plant life and human lungs, often attributed to preventable smoke, are in reality due to the non-preventable sulphuric acid as the active agent of destruction. This is produced from the coal during the process of combustion. It eats everything. Nothing escapes its voracity. It bites the bark off trees, ruins iron fencing, crumbles stone buildings, and at the present moment is eating the stone work of St. Paul and Westminster Cathedrals as well as the granite of our new skyscrapers."[9] Reformers called for stringent ordinances against burning trash and for the compulsory use in industry of antipollution devices. But these widely touted devices were often only partial cures for pollution, and were most effective on small

[6] "Fortunes That Have Literally Gone Up in Smoke," *Current Opinion* 54 (January, 1913): 71–73.

[7] Smithsonian Institution, *Annual Report, 1895* (Washington: Government Printing Office, 1896), pp. 135–287, contains three long essays on the composition of air and its effects on humans in several countries and major cities. See also "The Atmospheric Crisis with Which Civilization Is Threatened," *Current Literature* 43 (September, 1907): 331–332.

[8] "Why Smoke Is Injurious," *Literary Digest* 45 (November 30, 1912): 1007–1008; Sydney A. Dunham, "The Air We Breathe," *Chautauquan* 23 (May, 1896): 143–146; "The Smoke Nuisance," *Outlook* 71 (July 19, 1902): 710–711.

[9] Matthew Nelson, "Smoke Abatement in Cincinnati," *American City* 2 (January, 1910): 8–10.

equipment. Technology to control massive air pollution was not available. Most such equipment took care of only one aspect of smoke pollution, or merely laundered soot from the smoke column, leaving noxious steam and invisible gases. And the more complex such devices became, the less effective they often were in the hands of unskilled or uninterested workmen. By 1907, more laws on municipal statute books dealt with air pollution than with any other subject. But enforcement varied greatly from city to city and season to season, especially since inspectors were usually political appointees, often open to bribery.[10]

The general propaganda against air pollution emphasized needless waste, hidden maintenance costs, and dangers to health. But the average city dweller thought of dirty air as an unsightly inconvenience. It left rings on collars, dirtied wash on the line, made eyes smart, and discolored buildings. In Pittsburgh, "the mourning town," many people wore dark clothing as a defense against falling soot. But efforts to control air pollution encountered some ironic obstacles. The smoke pouring from factory stacks symbolized prosperity to both worker and owner. Smoke marked a town "on the go." Smoking factory chimneys appeared on elaborate stock and bond certificates to symbolize prosperity; there were even a few such scenes on national currency. And many householders would have resisted efforts to eliminate the

---

[10] Hollis Godfrey, "The Air of the City," *Atlantic Monthly* 102 (July, 1908): 62–71; Raymond C. Benner, "The Cost of an Industrial Nuisance," *American City* 8 (May, 1913): 496–497; A. W. Gibbs, "The Smoke Nuisance and the Railroads, Considered from the Economical and Geological Standpoint," *Scientific American Supplement* 738 (April 24, 1909): 258–259; George E. Walsh, "Smokeless Cities of Today," *Harper's Weekly* 51 (August 3, 1907): 1139; "Fortunes That Have Literally Gone up in Smoke," *Current Opinion* 54 (January, 1913): 71–73.

cheap coal and fuel oil that permitted millions to have central heating.[11]

Garbage was the most striking evidence of man's new relationship to the environment. Steadily increasing affluence, especially in urban areas, created waste materials that were difficult and expensive to dispose of. The rising standard of living was reflected in higher consumption of food, especially of meats, fruits, and fresh vegetables, whose remains posed new disposal problems.

The American passion for personal cleanliness was easily transferred to the trash problem. Trained experts joined reformers to agitate for a litter-free environment. Litter was an easy mark since it was an eyesore, fire hazard, and disease producer. Trained sanitation engineers rapidly professionalized their staffs and took advantage of technology. The sanitation worker's white suit, which symbolized cleanliness and order, became as familiar as the physician's smock or the scientist's apron.[12] Leaders in the field cooperated with the police in notifying residents of new regulations and ingeniously employed children and the school system to promote public concern for controlling trash.[13]

In small towns an incinerator or open dump usually sufficed for heavy wastes. But the disposal of huge quantities of "domestic rejectamenta" in cities required more formidable means.[14] A

[11] "Pittsburgh's Smoke Bill," *Scientific American* 110 (February 21, 1914): 154; "Home Fires," ibid. 121 (July 19, 1919): 60.

[12] Waring, *Modern Methods of Sewage Disposal*, p. 116.

[13] George E. Waring, Jr., "The Cleaning of a Great City," *McClure's Magazine* 9 (September, 1897): 911–924.

[14] George E. Waring, Jr., "Great Business Operations, Part 3: The Utilization of City Garbage," *Cosmopolitan Magazine* 24 (February, 1898): 404–412; John McGaw Woodbury, "The Wastes of a Great City," *Scribner's Monthly* 34 (October, 1903): 387–400. H. R. Crohurst, "Municipal Wastes:

survey of 150 cities and towns in the mid-nineties revealed a high degree of organization and sophistication in waste disposal.[15] Cities near large bodies of water or flowing rivers generally dumped processed waste into the water. Prevailing scientific theory held that most treated matter would be purified, and that moderate amounts of it helped fish reproduction.[16] Only a few experts realized that organic waste could overfeed lakes and rivers. Knowledge of the effects of new chemicals on marine life was imperfect.

Administrators were chiefly concerned to avoid lawsuits from cities downstream, or to prevent inshore dumping which aroused citizen ire: "Probably not much offensive garbage escapes the fish and action of the waves, but enough of this accompanies the straw, paper, boxes, cans, etc., with which the shore is often heavily lined, to have very much the same sentimental effect that a solid mass of garbage would have. In any event, the result is very disfiguring and very annoying to frequenters of the beaches and to owners of shore property."[17] Such commentators were usually concerned with the effects of dumping on property values rather than upon marine ecology.

Sanitary landfills were another innovation in waste treatment. If not properly supervised, these became breeding grounds for

---

Their Character, Collection, Disposal," United States Public Health Service *Bulletin* 107 (October, 1920): 1–98, offers comprehensive coverage and analysis of methods of disposal and of available technology. There is an exhaustive bibliography.

[15] Rudolph Hering, "The Vexed Question of Garbage Disposal," *Engineering Magazine* 13 (June, 1897): 392–398.

[16] Ibid.

[17] George E. Waring, Jr., "The Disposal of a City's Waste," *North American Review* 161 (July, 1895): 49–56.

insects and rodents and contaminated adjacent waters after rain-storms. But proper landfill was a popular method of disposal, since it created new land for development. Of course, this increased growth, consumption, and waste. Wastes that did not go to water or landfill were processed through new high-intensity furnaces, whose smoke was an ironic salute to progress.

The most sophisticated waste-reduction systems operated with predictable American efficiency. Collectors gathered certain kinds of garbage on stated days, for careful sorting, which often involved some recycling. Food scraps might go to a municipal piggery or be sold to farmers. Some paper, cardboard, rags, and bottles were reused. But economics and the desire to lower tax rates, rather than a concern for recycling, dictated this.

Thrift combined with necessity in some older attitudes, which incidentally reduced waste. Cities and towns were a bit cleaner, for instance, thanks to the wastepaper dealer, ragpicker, used-furniture man, and bottle collector. In humbler homes, many things were reused. Rags went into rugs and quilts; bottles were reused for decoration and home canning; and paper found a multitude of uses. But, again, economics rather than a sense of scarcity motivated this. Materials were still generally more expensive than labor, and it was feasible to recycle some articles.

Both scientists and entrepreneurs developed many uses for solid wastes. Food scraps became animal feed or fertilizer. Some trash was compressed into building bricks; ashes were sold to make cinder blocks, paving materials, and fireproof flooring. Glass, sawdust, and metals went to the scrap market.[18] Scientists experimented with burning garbage to heat buildings and gener-

[18] "How Waste Is Turned into Money," *Scientific American* 95 (October 6, 1906): 245–246.

Antinoise agitation produced a large body of laws, especially on local levels, which were more honored in the newspapers than in the courts. Officials simply could not control the great variety of noisemakers, ranging from shouting fruit peddlers to riverboat whistles, cracking whips, and a great variety of industrial bedlam.

Efforts to understand and control environmental changes were often fraught with irony. The horse, for instance, who did most of society's brute labor, was the most obvious polluter of any city street or country lane. Experts developed methods of disposing of huge quantities of manure, especially hazardous in busy cities. Some manure was sold to farmers, or used to fertilize city parks and gardens; some was rendered down for mineral content. But technology soon made it cheaper to buy chemical fertilizers than to use animal waste. Most manure was simply hosed into sewer systems, or collected and dumped into bodies of water, where it often affected marine life.

Small wonder that people welcomed the internal-combustion engine as a deliverance from the hazards of horse manure. The automobile offered "the feelings of independence, the freedom from timetables, from fixed and inflexible routes, from the proximity of other human beings than one's chosen companions; the ability to go where and when one wills, to linger and stop where the country is beautiful and the way pleasant, or to rush through unattractive surroundings, to select the best places to sleep and eat; and the satisfaction that comes from a knowledge that one need ask favors or accommodation from no one, or trespass on anybody's property or privacy."[24]

[24] Larry McKilwin, "Keeping the Land Yacht Shipshape," *Harper's Weekly* 53 (January 2, 1909): 10. For general background on the automobile, see

The automobile was "the servant of civilization," combining most elements in the American dream of freedom, variety, and power.[25] The highways it needed would develop the nation, unite rural and urban areas, and improve the individual through travel.[26] The automobile would also reduce the use of resources, since it produced more energy per cost unit than did the horse. The internal-combustion engine would revolutionize mass transit and alleviate street congestion.

Above all, it would end man's dependence on the horse's brute labor, another sign of "civilized progress." And the horse seemed a major stumbling block to that progress. There were 120,000 horses in New York City in 1908; some 83,000 in Chicago; 12,000 in Detroit; and 5,000 in Columbus, Ohio, backed by an elaborate and costly system of maintenance. The automobile would eliminate street sweeping, stabling, and veterinary costs.[27] It would banish the horse manure which was a major irritant and danger to city living. The average horse produced over 15 pounds of manure daily. One enterprising reporter, revealing the characteristic national passion for both trivial facts and grandiose conclusions, estimated that the city of Rochester's 25,000 horses produced an annual pile of manure 175 feet high, covering an

---

John B. Rae, *The American Automobile: A Brief History* (Chicago: University of Chicago Press, 1965). James J. Flink, *America Adopts the Automobile, 1895–1910* (Cambridge: MIT Press, 1970), is an outstanding work that discusses the automobile's sociological, economic, and cultural meanings in the period.

[25] "The Automobile As Servant of Civilization," *Arena* 27 (January, 1902): 93–98.

[26] "Good Roads and Good Morals," *Chautauquan* 24 (December, 1896): 345–346, is a typical discussion of the general social advantages of improved roads.

[27] Flink, *America Adopts the Automobile,* pp. 88–100.

acre, which hosted 16 billion flies. Dead animals, like car hulks of the future, were a major disposal and sanitation problem. In 1880, the city of New York had to move an estimated 15,000 carcasses.[28] To the horseless carriage's champions final freedom from fly-borne diseases seemed assured. "With the horse off the streets, the fly must follow him," a prominent New York physician said. "It will not be where the horse is not. . . . The horseless carriage will greatly reduce the death rate in our cities."[29]

The automobile's pneumatic tires would also reduce noise. The clatter of horses' hoofs, scrape of iron wheels, cries of drivers, cracking whips, and bloody accidents would stop.[30]

Few commentators doubted the automobile's general beneficence; none foresaw the congestion, waste, and air pollution it would bring. Only a few saw that it would further congest the cities, or that the road system would radiate heat and cause rainwater to run off too rapidly.[31] The rush to adopt the automobile was understandable, but well illustrated how unpredictable side-effects accompanied the solutions offered for many environmental problems.

Enthusiasm for the internal-combustion engine symptomized efforts to increase and purify energy sources. Scientists did not foresee an immediate power shortage, given the country's enor-

[28] "Horseless Carriages and Sanitation," *Scientific American* 74 (January 18, 1896): 36; Harold Bolce, "The Horse vs. Health," *American Magazine* 11 (May, 1908): 532–538; Joel A. Tarr, "Urban Pollution: Many Long Years Ago," *American Heritage* 22 (October, 1971): 65–69, 106.

[29] Quoted in William F. Small, *Third Pollution* (New York: Praeger, 1971), p. 77.

[30] "The Horseless Carriage and Public Health," *Scientific American* 80 (February 18, 1899): 98.

[31] Dunham, "The Air We Breathe," pp. 143–146.

mous reserves of coal and oil. But they studied the possibilities of using the sun's rays and ocean tides to generate power.[32]

Electricity seemed to be the power of the future. It would reduce air pollution and noise,[33] and would eliminate a great deal of drudgery in the home, thus increasing leisure time. "It is an interesting fact that the needs of the household were the first objects of our American inventors," a scientist noted.[34] Interesting, but predictable, given the national penchant for ease, gadgetry, and luxury. Electricity seemed clean, safe, and far removed from brute labor. It was scientifically progressive, with enough magical qualities to be glamorous. Few people worried about using huge quantities of fossil fuel, in the absence of falling water, to generate current. Hydroelectric facilities also required direct intervention against environmental balance with the construction of dams and creation of lakes. Still fewer people worried about the proliferation of power-consuming gadgets, or foresaw the whole new category of eye pollution that came with telephone poles, wires, and lighted billboards.

Advertising, a booming aspect of the new economy, became a double environmental threat. It promoted wasteful consumption, and it was itself a new form of pollution. Billboards sprang up everywhere. Brochures and expanded newspapers filled with advertisements ended up as waste or litter. Promoters played on Americans' long-standing love of fancy packaging, and many

[32] Nathaniel Southgate Shaler, *Man and the Earth* (Chautauqua, N.Y.: Chautauqua Press, 1905), p. 41.

[33] Elihu Thompson, "Future Electrical Development," *New England Magazine* 6 (July, 1892): 623–635, is a good summary of the expectations accorded electrical power.

[34] Shaler, *The United States of America*, II, 808. See also George Heli Guy, "Electricity in the Household," *Chautauquan* 26 (October, 1897): 50–54.

homely items came swathed in art work worthy of a higher cause. Urban buyers liked stylish packaging, and such elegance linked rural consumers to a more glamorous world. The entire tendency promoted litter, waste of paper, and the introduction of chemicals and inks into the environment.[35]

The relation of population to waste and pollution was misunderstood. The rate of growth seemed to be stabilizing, and late Victorians were concerned about "race suicide" in technologically advanced nations. Few Americans believed the country would become overcrowded. The needs and energies of an expanding population were the basis of national affluence. Nor did the food supply seem inadequate, especially since farmers complained of overproduction and falling prices. Science and technology were discovering new ways to increase crop yields and to use marginal lands. The seas would feed future generations, and new forms of concentrated foodstuffs would prevent world famine. In any event, starvation would never threaten the United States.

Many Americans understood the symptoms of environmental damage and were concerned about the quality of life in an industrial society. But few grasped the subtleties involved in ecological balances which had long-term effects on man's very survival.

[35] Sylvester Baxter, "The Nuisance of Advertising," *Century Magazine* 73 (January, 1907): 419–430; Burton J. Hendrick, "The Bill-Board Abomination," *Leslie's Monthly* 60 (May, 1905): 85–91; "Unit Association for Bill-board Suppression," *American City* 1 (November, 1909): 132–133. I do not mean to imply that advertising *necessarily* produced eye pollution. And wasteful and unesthetic advertising materials and methods helped provoke the City Beautiful movement, which aimed to plan and beautify streets, lighting systems, parks, and so forth, keeping them free from advertising. But "advertising pollution" reflected a historic and deeply rooted American indifference to haste; an acceptance of temporary expedients in the hope of permanent solutions; and an aversion to control of private activities.

A few men, like George Perkins Marsh, warned that "man is everywhere a disturbing agent. Wherever he plants his foot, the harmonies of nature are turned to discords."[36] Scientists, like Nathaniel Southgate Shaler, tried to explain and popularize ecology through courses and lectures on geology and human geography. But a certain pessimism tinged the writings of even so dedicated a man as Shaler. The "lowlier individuals" in the life chain struggled to accommodate themselves merely to survive and procreate. "With man, however, bacause of his ever-expanding ideals and the desires they breed, the reconciliation is almost infinitely more difficult to effect. It is, indeed, unaccomplishable. Our kind may fairly be distinguished as a new type of being, one in which the movement toward adjustment with surroundings is . . . a curve which constantly approaches the straight line, but can never attain it. With each advance in this process, new desires originate, so that the finish to the process is infinitely remote, to be won only when he has, in the largest sense of the word, comprehended the realm."[37] Sophisticated analysts could only hope that man's intelligence would arrest his destructiveness and permit him to develop technology to remedy environmental damage.

The loss of visible natural resources like topsoil, trees, and minerals was the most dramatic evidence of environmental damage. But animals in danger of extinction also provoked considerable public discussion. Informed critics granted the inevitable demise of some marginal species which were dangerous or in-

[36] George Perkins Marsh, *Man and Nature* (Cambridge, Mass.: Harvard University Press, 1965), p. 36; and David Lowenthal, *George Perkins Marsh: Versatile Vermonter* (New York: Columbia University Press, 1965), pp. 246–276. Marsh's book was first published in 1864.

[37] Shaler, *Man and the Earth*, pp. 159–160, 191; see also his *Nature and Man in America* (New York: Charles Scribner's Sons, 1891).

convenient to man. But aroused groups took the lead in trying to ban hunting of some animals for their skins, feathers, or ivory.

Shaler took the loftiest grounds in defending dwindling species. Science, he argued, did not know the exact place of every creature in the evolutionary chain. Nature likely would replace extinct species with an unknown quantity. Many animals, also, became important to man unexpectedly; the lowly horse and cow furnished cultures for smallpox and diphtheria serums. The depredations of every species, and their effects on total natural balance, were poorly understood. Removal of one allegedly unimportant or threatening animal often aided a more dangerous one.

Shaler was acutely conscious of posterity's judgments on what Americans did in this area. "Each of these kinds we destroy is absolutely irreplaceable," he wrote, "no record we can make of it will be satisfactory to the learning of a thousand years hence."[38] He and others repeatedly emphasized a special American mission to safeguard species. This, like liberal works in economics and politics, would prove that America was better than the Old World. Shaler eloquently called on Americans to display sensitivity as well as self-interest in abandoning the "childish notion that the marvellous life of this world is fitly to be taken as a toy for man, to be carelessly rent away with his plow, or slain for his diversion. This establishment of a truly civilized state of mind, as regards man's duty by those creatures of all degree who share life with him, is the necessary foundation for such conduct as will keep our race and time from shame in the ages to come."[39]

---

[38] Shaler, *Man and the Earth*, pp. 199–200, 207; Marsh, *Man and Nature*, pp. 37 ff., 86–87.

[39] Shaler, *Man and the Earth*, p. 208.

Government at various levels watched over some endangered species. The bison and some seals enjoyed federal protection. Vultures, plumed birds, beavers, some elk and antelope were protected. Yet the policy was contradictory. Government agencies supported extinction programs against various large cats, such rodents as the prairie dog, and wolves, all of which were highly significant in maintaining ecological balance. Many species did not in fact threaten man.[40] This concern for endangered species was symptomatic of a growing official interest in the en-

[40] The use of pesticides and predator controls is a technical subject outside the scope of this essay. The Department of Agriculture developed pesticides, especially for cereal crops and fruits, in response to pressure from agricultural interests. Most of these, such as "Paris green" and "London purple," contained arsenic, lead, or petroleum derivatives. A great variety of spraying mechanisms were available. Various government agencies also experimented successfully with natural controls based on biological balances. Indeed, many farm experts doubted that chemicals would ever eradicate pests, and hoped for breakthroughs in biological experimentations. The ladybug was imported to attack orchard insects, and several species of birds were used to consume pests. Farmers were notified about the beneficial work of birds and animals in transplating seeds from one locale to another and in promoting soil enrichment and ground cover. Printed bulletins and traveling agricultural agents kept farmers advised of which birds and animals deserved protection. See Marsh, *Man and Nature*, pp. 79 ff.; "Work on Insects from Abroad," *Yearbook of the United States Department of Agriculture, 1902* (Washington: Government Printing Office, 1903), pp. 80–90. T. S. Palmer, "Some Benefits the Farmer May Receive from Game Protection," *Yearbook of the United States Department of Agriculture, 1904* (Washington: Government Printing Office, 1905), pp. 509–520. There is no full history of the subject, but James C. Whorton, "Insecticide Spray Residues and Public Health, 1865–1938," *Bulletin of the History of Medicine* 45 (May–June, 1971): 219–241, has some excellent information and analysis. L. O. Howard, *A History of Applied Entomology* (Washington: Smithsonian Institution Miscellaneous Collections no. 84, 1930), covers world developments in a cursory fashion. There is also some useful information in Aaron J. Ihde, "Pests and Disease Controls," in Melvin Kranzberg and Carroll W. Pursell, Jr., eds., *Technology in Western Civilization*, 2 vols. (New York: Oxford University Press, 1967), II, 369–385.

vironment. The federal government studied general environmental problems through its bureaus, the Fish and Game Commission (1871), the Geological Survey (1879), and various groups under the Smithsonian Institution. By the turn of the century, national and local agencies had made elaborate studies of water resources, reclamation, wildlife, and natural wealth.

Such private groups as the Sierra Club (1892) and the National Audubon Society (1905) lobbied with officials and the public. Specialists in engineering, earth sciences, city planning, and architecture were especially vocal in discussing environmental issues. Their professional journals and societies generated information, suggestions, and publicity—in turn popularized in many magazines and newspapers.

Critics obtained a great deal of regulatory legislation, especially on local levels, but many laws became dead letters. The number of individuals involved, the great range of activities, and the power of special interests soon enfolded the conservation crusade. Private and public bodies became information gatherers, often oriented toward the activities they were supposed to oversee. Most proponents of environmental control relied on technology, and the public steadily adjusted to industrial life. Reformers shared the prevailing national ethic that rested on efficient production and consumption. They simply wished to rationalize resource use and remove special interests from politics. Like most Americans, only a few leaders accepted the idea of limited natural wealth.

This first generation of Americans to live with industrialism responded quickly and optimistically to environmental challenges. In a purely technical sense— in controlling water purity, sewage, waste disposal—they managed most problems well.

The damage was greatest in misuse of natural raw materials and soils. The chemical revolution that threatened the world's water and air had not yet fully arrived. While there was a developing environmental problem, it was not yet of crisis proportions. It was also closest to city dwellers who were underrepresented in government. But in the end, ironically enough, the obvious wealth of national resources delayed full consciousness of genuine crisis.

The most unfortunate result of the generation's confrontation with the environment did not lie in lack of imagination or concern, but in the failure to question basic attitudes that promoted waste and inhibited social planning. Americans continued to alternate between the desire to subdue and exploit nature, and the determination to reinstate her fancied security.[41] They seldom perceived general ecological principles, however willingly they attacked single symptoms. Nor did they alter the long-standing American aversion to planning. Americans always found it hard to surrender the goal of private gain to the ideal of orderly development that threatened to bring government regulation.

Americans always believed they enjoyed the protection of a special providence, which in turn guaranteed the beneficent results of their individualism. Their historic openness to innovation, a persistent curiosity, and energy sustained the immense

[41] Roderick Nash has discussed these attitudes and conflicting aims in three recent works: *Wilderness and the American Mind* (New Haven: Yale University Press, 1967); *The American Environment: Readings in the History of Conservation* (Reading, Mass.: Addison-Wesley, 1969), and "The State of Environmental History," in Herbert J. Bass, ed., *The State of American History* (Chicago: Quadrangle Books, 1970), pp. 249–260. The literature on conservation is large, but Samuel P. Hays, *Conservation and the Gospel of Efficiency* (Cambridge, Mass.: Harvard University Press, 1955), remains the best analytical overview.

economic growth that made the country and its people the richest on earth by 1900. The new seemed better than the old; the untried begged trying; the possible should be done. Haste was not an error, since something better would come along on the line of automatic progress. These same values, often so healthy in industry, science, and thought, were potentially disastrous when tied to consumerism based on waste.

America also rested on the ideal of abundance. The hope and apparent possibility of attaining affluence underlay the stubborn individualism and the aversion to planning which cut down through every layer of society. To accept, or even to concede, the idea of ultimate scarcity would require reevaluation of the whole national ethic and way of life.

The problems this first industrial generation faced were new; advice was often conflicting, even among scientists. The challenges also seemed technical, and the era had great faith in problem-solving as a way of avoiding general regulation. But, above all, with a population of 75,000,000 in 1900, and of 105,000,000 in 1920, America seemed permanently spacious, her resources and will as limitless as the inherited promise of American life.